THE WAR AGAINST PROGRESS

About the Author:

Herbert E. Meyer is an associate editor of FORTUNE. His articles, essays, and lectures on both foreign and domestic affairs have made him one of this country's most respected political and economic commentators. Mr. Meyer was born in Brooklyn, New York, in 1945, and is a graduate of Brooklyn College. He is a member of the Council on Foreign Relations.

The War Against Progress

BY

HERBERT E. MEYER

STORM KING PUBLISHERS INC.

NEW YORK

FIRST EDITION

Library of Congress Catalog Card Number: 79-66668
ISBN: 0-935166-00-9

So much of what I've accomplished—including publication of this book—would not have been possible without the help and encouragement of my brother, Edward.

Table of Contents

1

A New Kind
of Conflict

CHAPTER ONE

We are in the midst of a war. However, it is not the kind of war that we are used to fighting. In this war there are no battleships, no infantry platoons, no airplanes, no bombed-out villages or cities, no refugees fleeing for their lives down crowded roads. And it is precisely because this war is so different, and so difficult to see, that it is so dangerous. We may very well lose it even before we become aware that we are in it. Yet the war has been going on now for more than a decade. Its battles have raged from one end of the United States to the other, and lately the fighting has begun to spread. In just the last two or three years, there have been skirmishes in Great Britain, France, West Germany, Austria, Italy, Belgium, Switzerland, Spain, Portugal, parts of Scandinavia, Canada, and Japan. It is the war against progress, and the price of losing it will be more destruction and human misery, for more people in more countries, than any previous war has ever brought.

At first blush, the notion that we are in the midst of a war against progress may seem preposterous. After all, it's hard to believe that anyone in his or her right mind would struggle to undermine such an obviously good thing as progress itself. Moreover, no one has actually come right out and said, in so many words, that he is against progress. But then, no one ever will. Like peace, progress is the sort of thing that everyone always insists he is for—in principle. However, it is one thing to profess support for a principle, and quite another to actually pursue the policies required to turn that principle into an accomplished fact. A country is not in favor of peace merely because its leaders say so, after all, if at the same time that country is arming to its teeth and sending guerilla troops on nightly raids across the border. And in this same sense, a country is not in favor of progress merely because its leaders say so, if at the same time that country is pursuing policies that either reduce the rate at which progress can be made or that prevent it altogether.

Today an army that opposes progress is fighting to inflict its policies and its philosophy on the United States. Among the soldiers in this small but powerful army are many of our elected political leaders, many of the high-level bureaucrats who administer the daily business of our federal, state, and local government agencies, and many of our country's unelected, unappointed social activists. This last group includes university professors, authors, journalists, many of those part-time and professional lobbyists who insist that their only purpose is to "make things better," and even entertainers such as movie stars and recording artists.

As these people see it, the United States has now come to the end of its spectacular journey through history. After more than two centuries of scientific discovery, technological innovation, and economic growth, we have gone about as far as we can safely go. Our scientists and our engineers have created a world that is too risky, too dangerous, too dirty to tolerate. Our corporations and our business executives have created a society that is too materialistic, too unequal, too unfair to accept. Indeed, these opponents of progress warn, we could not continue to go forward even if we wanted to. For we are running out of natural resources. We are even running out of room. So—say the enemies of progress—we must set aside the naive notion that our future is limited only by our imagination, by our talent for innovating, by our willingness to work, and by our tolerance of financial inequality, of environmental change, of personal risk. And we must once and for all abandon the idea that things can and will get better if only we keep on trying. Things won't get better no matter how hard we try, because we have already pushed and pulled and puffed our economy to its bursting point. From now on we must learn to live with less. Those who have too much will have to give some up to those who have too little. In short, we have gone as far as we can go. We have got to stop now before it is too late—before we go too far and bring the whole thing crashing down on top of us.

Moreover—the opponents of progress add—we should not be the slightest bit upset by the notion that our country's day is done. Indeed, they say, we should be thankful for it. For one thing, learning to live with less will do us all some good; small is beautiful. And in any case our country has become much too powerful, much too technologically advanced, much too heavily industrialized for the good of mankind. Our military power is a primary cause of instability around the globe, these people insist, for clearly it is we who are driving the arms race. Our economic power is a major obstacle to Third World countries that are struggling to overcome poverty, these people argue, for clearly it is we who are keeping the Third World poor by using up so much of our planet's limited resources. And because U.S. multinational corporations produce so many products in so many countries, these people claim, our country stands condemned as history's most irresponsible polluter. If only we will pull in our horns and turn inward—if only we will stop trying to be the biggest and the strongest in everything—the world will be a better, cleaner, safer place for everyone.

To those who share this point of view, there is only one way to save ourselves and the rest of humanity from the U.S. Our country's rate of progress must be forced down from its present level. And it is to accomplish this objective that the army of political leaders, bureaucrats, and assorted social activists is fighting to frustrate and delay the various efforts that are now being made to keep our country moving forward through the years ahead. Naturally, these individuals also believe that the world would be a better place if the U.S. rate of progress could be kept down permanently. And it is to accomplish this second objective that their army is fighting to steer our country onto a wholly new course. More precisely, it is fighting to convert the U.S. from the world's most dynamic and powerful industrial civilization into a quiet, clean, safe refuge in which there will be no growth, no pollution, no financial inequality, and no personal risk. In other words, no possibility of progress.

The strategy adopted by the enemies of progress to win their struggle is a subtle and extremely clever one. It is to profess support for the principle of progress—to sing its praises as often and as loudly as possible—while at the same time to stop progress by systematically undermining its components. Economic growth, technological innovation, scientific research—these are the components of progress. These are the engines that drive a country forward. And today all three of these complicated and costly processes are under attack as never before in our country's history. First, the enemies of progress are fighting overtly, in specific places and with as much publicity as possible, to stop specific projects that have already been started. Some of these projects are absolutely necessary for the U.S. economy to grow. Others involve the deployment of new technologies. And still others are crucial to the advancement of certain key branches of science. At the same time, the enemies of progress are fighting covertly, and with as little publicity as possible, to limit the number of progressive projects that will be proposed or actually started in the future. They are doing this by pursuing policies and programs which make these projects so complicated, so expensive, and so unprofitable that individuals, corporations, and universities will be reluctant or unable to launch them in the first place.

Many of today's most newsworthy events in fact are part of the war against progress. For example, the campaign by environmentalist and other groups to delay the completion of nuclear and even non-nuclear power facilities—a campaign that began long before the accident at Three Mile Island—is part of the larger effort to slow down the current U.S. economic growth rate.

Without new energy facilities, our industries will be unable to expand, and by doing so to create enough new jobs for all those Americans who need or want to work. The campaign to stop oil companies from drilling for oil and building refineries—a campaign that has led directly to our present gasoline shortage—is part of the larger effort to force Americans to live with less. Today's rapidly spreading campaign to limit the physical growth of our country's most attractive towns and cities is part of the larger effort to slow down our current rate of social progress. Without new houses and apartments in our better neighborhoods, Americans who are now living in urban slums will be trapped where they are; there will literally be no room anywhere else even for those who do manage to climb the economic ladder. And the campaign to restrict one of today's most promising branches of scientific inquiry—recombinant DNA research, also called gene-splicing—is part of a larger effort to hobble the U.S. scientific community, whose accomplishments have contributed so much to our country's success.

High tax rates, staggering government deficits, regulations that fairly strangle our corporations and our universities in red tape, the recent outcry over corporate profits, the general assault on wealth—these too are part of the war against progress. They are part of a long-range effort to cripple the U.S., and then to keep it from ever making a full recovery, by siphoning out of our economy as much money as possible. Money, of course, is the fuel of progress. The smaller the amount of money that remains in people's pockets to do with as they please—and the less this money is worth—the more slowly a country's economy will grow, the fewer technological innovations it will develop and deploy, and the less scientific research it will be able to conduct. Siphon out enough money from enough pockets for a long enough period of time, and eventually the economic engines will grind to a halt; their most delicate parts will burn out or be crushed beyond repair. And this is what the enemies of progress have in mind to do. For when our country's economic engines have ground to a halt, public support for our capitalist, free enterprise system will diminish. Instead of trying to fix it, we will likely vote to replace our "broken" system with a new one; a system in which government, rather than the marketplace, will be dominant.

Despite their efforts and their many victories, the enemies of progress have not yet won their war. Most Americans continue to favor robust economic growth, rapid technological innovation, and unfettered scientific research. They continue to accept the costs, the inconveniences, the inequalities, and the very considerable risks of making progress. They understand that the alternative to moving forward is not standing still, but falling backward. Most importantly, many Americans who belong to this progressive majority are willing to fight. Indeed, in some instances they have even managed to defeat the enemies of progress on the battlefield. For example, the June 1978 victory of California's Proposition 13, to slash property taxes in that state by a whopping 57 percent, was a stunning setback for those politicians, bureaucrats, and social activists who for years have been holding back that state's economy by siphoning out of it as much money as they can. And in April 1979, just three weeks after the accident at Three Mile Island, voters in Austin, Texas, rejected pleas by anti-nuclear activists and voted to continue funding construction of a nearby nuclear power plant.

But victories like these have been few and far between. Obviously they are welcome but just as obviously they are not sufficient. The enemies of progress are too well organized, and they have gained too much momentum, to be stopped by occasional setbacks, administered every so often in one place or another. The job will require a carefully planned, across-the-board counterattack; one that is designed to sweep the enemies of progress completely off the battlefield, and to discredit their philosophy to the point where it can never again be used to raise an army strong enough to start another war.

There is not much time left in which to get organized. According to a growing number of important statistics, the U.S. has already begun to move forward at a slower rate than ever before. And today there is an alarming number of little-publicized but key indicators which suggest that in fact this loss of momentum is by no means temporary. Indeed the evidence is overwhelming that our gallop, so to speak, has now become a walk. It is impossible to escape the conclusion that if the war against progress continues to rage for too much longer, our walk will soon become a crawl. Then we will stop moving forward altogether, and finally we will begin to slip backward toward our ultimate destruction. And the decline of the U.S. will be a calamitous event that very few other countries, and none of our allies, will be able to survive.

It is scarcely an exaggeration to describe the situation as critical. When you stop to consider what progress really means, and then to analyze what policies and attitudes are required to actually make it happen, you begin to understand how close the enemies of progress have already come to a final victory.

CHAPTER

2

What Progress Means and What It Takes

CHAPTER TWO

Progress is the expansion of opportunity. It is the process that enables more and more people to lead whatever sorts of lives they want; that enables people to make decisions for themselves concerning how to live, where to live, what kind of work to do, and even how to spend leisure time. Can we afford to get married now, or must we wait a while? Can we continue to live in our home town, near our friends and relatives, or must we move into the city to find work? Should I tell my boss to get lost the next time he orders me to work overtime without pay, or must I keep my mouth shut and do as he says because the job market is rotten and I can't afford to get fired? Should we buy a piano and start the kids on lessons? Should we spend our summer holiday puttering around the house, or can we afford to take a trip?

Questions like these are vitally important. The answers to them form the shape of our daily lives, and we all want the opportunity to make the choices that in turn will make us happy. When we say that a country is making progress, we mean that more and more of its people are becoming free to actually make these choices for themselves, rather than be trapped in circum-stances, places, jobs, and styles of life they don't like, by forces that are beyond their power to control.

Now it so happens that there is only one way to expand opportunity—in other words, to make progress. You do it by creating jobs. This is by no means a controversial opinion or even a theory. It is a fact of economic and political life, and therefore it is just as valid for a capitalist democracy, a socialist dictatorship, or any other kind of system that has ever been tried or that you can possibly imagine. The more jobs that are available, the greater the opportunity for more people to live the sorts of lives they want; the sorts of lives that will make them happy. There is only one exception to this axiom. If you happen to be one of those people who is content to muddle along at the bare subsistence level of existence, the number of jobs available and the variety of jobs available are not expecially important. In fact, they are completely irrelevant. You can lay claim to a half-acre of land that nobody else wants, grow your own food, build your own shelter out of whatever materials you can find, capture and skin wild animals for clothing, and boil their fat to make candles and soap. You can also expect to drop dead of exhaustion or disease before you reach forty. But you will never need a job. A job is necessary only if you want more than this out of life.

Most people, of course, do want more out of life than merely to survive. And most of the things that people want cost money. For example, we want decent apartments or houses in pleasant neighborhoods, where shopping is convenient and where the kids can play outside without getting hurt in the rubble of burned-out

16

buildings or getting beat up for loose change by desperate drug addicts. We want to furnish our houses or apartments comfortably —not just with items we absolutely need such as beds and a kitchen table, but with items we want for relaxation such as a stereo set or a piano or a ping-pong table for the basement. We want to be able to afford a car that looks nice and that starts ninety-nine mornings out of a hundred. And we want enough spare cash after the monthly bills are paid so we can go out to dinner on Saturday, see the latest movies, join the local golf or tennis club, take a good vacation every summer, and still have enough in the bank account at Christmas to buy presents for everyone without going into hock. For those of us who did not have the foresight to choose wealthy parents, there is only one legal way to get our hands on enough money to live this comfortable but hardly extravagant sort of life. That is to earn the money by holding down a decent job. And you obviously cannot hold down a decent job if that job is not there to be held in the first place.

Most people do not work for the hell of it. They do not leap out of bed each morning and head for their factories, their offices, or their shops because the idea of working all day is more appealing to them than the idea of sleeping in. They do it because they want the reward they get for working; they want the money. And for these people, who comprise the overwhelming majority of the work force of this or any other country, the specific job is not too terribly important. What matters most is that the pay is right, the conditions decent, the hours reasonable, and the commute tolerable. It is only to the remaining, very tiny fraction of a country's population that the financial rewards of working are incidental, or at least of secondary importance. In this elite category are those very special, very gifted people who can be happy only if they are doing a very specific kind of work. These are the people—artists, musicians, scholars, fashion designers, and so forth—who get their satisfaction from performing their jobs, rather than from spending whatever money those jobs enable them to earn.

For these people even more than for the others, the opportunity to be happy depends utterly upon the number of jobs that can be created. Why? Because jobs for skilled and gifted people are always the most difficult jobs to create. Indeed, they can exist only in countries where there are plenty of jobs for ordinary people. For it is the ordinary people in any country who buy the goods and services that special people have to offer. Only in a country whose people are earning enough money to buy stereo sets and records, for example, can there be jobs for recording artists. Only in a country whose people can afford to buy paperback novels, can novelists make a living by staying home and writing them. And only in a country whose people are wealthy enough to buy more clothing than they absolutely need, can fashion designers stay in business by bringing out new styles every season.

The only way to expand opportunity—the only way to make progress—is to create jobs. There is just no other way to do it. Jobs make it possible for people to earn the money they need to live comfortably, which is all that the overwhelming majority of us wants to do. And for those of us who can be happy only if we are doing a very specific kind of work, the more ordinary jobs that exist the greater will be the chances of finding the work we want. Ironically, the ordinary jobs that most people hold down actually make possible the exciting jobs for those few who are sufficiently gifted and motivated to get them. It is important to emphasize this point because today there is a disturbing tendency among individuals with genuinely exciting and fulfilling jobs to consider themselves a thing apart from the rest of society; to look down their noses at people who work solely for the money. Individuals who feel this way, and there seem to be a lot of them teaching in our most prestigious universities and writing for our most popular newspapers and magazines, are more than snobs. They are economic imbeciles. Their own jobs would not survive for long without a healthy, growing economy to sustain them. Look around the world and you will find without exception that the most creative and culturally dynamic countries are also the wealthiest countries. It is not a coincidence.

Jobs are not natural things. One does not discover them lying on the bottom of streams, like nuggets of gold, or hidden underground like diamonds. They do not spring up like weeds in a garden. Jobs are artificial, so to speak. They must be created by people who know how to create them. And the business of creating jobs is one of the riskiest and most complicated in the world. It requires an enormous amount of intelligence, skill, ambition, common sense, and plain old-fashioned luck. Under the very best of circumstances, it is always an uphill battle to create a job; one is always more likely to fail than to succeed. Moreover, jobs are very delicate. Like orchids in a hothouse, they require intensive care and attention. Jobs die quickly if conditions are not just right; for instance if the market for a product collapses or if the price of a raw material rises too sharply. You must constantly make adjustments to compensate for changes that are impossible to anticipate or to prevent, such as a fire or a national recession. Make one wrong decision, or make a right decision too late, and the job you have created will shrivel up and die.

Jobs are created through the process of economic growth. They are, if you will, the by-product of this rather complicated process. For example, somebody with a lot of money in his pocket, or with access to a lot of money, decides to put up a new factory. So this ambitious individual—the precise word for him is entrepreneur—starts off by taking the obvious first step. He hires a construction firm. The owner of this construction firm then goes out and hires engineers, electricians, bricklayers, carpenters, and whatever other kinds of workers he will need to complete the project. Once these people are working and on the payroll, they have some money to spend. They want better-quality foods, better clothing, houses, cars, tennis lessons, movie tickets, and all the other goods and services that only money can buy. So the people who grow food, who make clothing, who build houses, who manufacture cars, who give tennis lessons, and who make movies now set out to actually provide these goods and services to the people who have been hired by the construction firm, and who are now earning enough money to buy the things they need or want.

Jobs create jobs. Soon all the people who are providing goods and services for employees of the construction firm are themselves earning enough money to buy the things they need or want. The farmer decides to buy a new suit. The tailor buys a house. The builder buys a car. The auto-worker joins the local tennis club. The tennis instructor takes his date to the movies, and the movie star uses his royalties to hire an architect to design a mansion in Beverly Hills. All of this, in turn, creates even more new jobs. For example, the tennis-equipment manufacturer and the architectural firms will now hire more and more people to help meet the growing demand for their products, and the local tennis club will hire a second instructor to give lessons to all the club's new members. And when the factory itself is at last completed, still more new jobs will be created for people to work in it and to produce whatever it is the factory was built to produce. So far, so good. Excellent, in fact. Jobs are being created all over the place. And with the money that people are able to earn by working at these jobs, they are increasingly able to afford the goods and services they want. Their standards of living are rising. More importantly, their opportunities to live where they want and how they want are expanding. In short, they are making progress. And they owe it all to that original decision by the entrepreneur to go out and build his factory.

Obviously, entrepreneurs are useful creatures. Indeed, they are absolutely vital to the business of making progress. But entrepreneurs are also ornery and very finicky creatures. They will not perform their function—that is, they will not make the investments that result in the creation of new jobs—merely because people want them to perform it. After all, one can hardly expect entrepreneurs to go out and build new factories for the sheer sport of it. Factories cost too much, they require a lot of time and energy to complete and then to operate successfully, and under the best imaginable circumstances the business of building and running factories is exceptionally difficult and frustrating. And neither can one ask entrepreneurs to go out and build new factories by appealing to their better natures; by begging them to do good for those who are less fortunate than themselves. Mind you, it would be wonderful if charity were sufficient motivation. But it never has been, it isn't now, and it never will be.

Entrepreneurs perform when it is in their own interest to perform. There is no other motivation powerful enough to make them do it. Entrepreneurs after all are human beings, subject to human weaknesses, and most of us are basically selfish. We do something because we want a reward for doing it, and the harder the thing is to do, the fatter the reward we expect for doing it. An entrepreneur will never start a new business for the sheer sport of it. When an entrepreneur wants a bit of sport, he can go to the races or throw a splashy party for his friends. And an entrepreneur will never start a new business out of a burning desire to help other people. When an entrepreneur wants to help those less fortunate than himself, he can donate to his favorite charity. An entrepreneur will start a new business only when he wants to make more money. Admittedly, this rather selfish motive is not one to uplift the spirits. However, it does uplift the incomes of an awful lot of ordinary people by creating jobs for them that otherwise would not exist. One need not love entrepreneurs to appreciate their value, and to recognize how critically important it is to create conditions that will entice them to perform their vital function.

Entrepreneurs need new technologies. This is the key to

success; this is the secret of it. After all, an entrepreneur can not make money by building a factory that manufactures the very same product that is already being manufactured somewhere else, and in the very same way that this product is being manufactured elsewhere. The owners of those other factories will not step aside politely to make room for a new competitor. They will step in, so to speak, to try and blow him right out of business. And they will probably succeed. The only way an entrepreneur can hope to make money from a new factory is to have something extra going for him. This something extra is a technological innovation. With a new technology, an entrepreneur can manufacture a product that simply is not being manufactured anywhere else. Or he can manufacture an existing product better and more cheaply than his competitors.

Put another way, a technological innovation gives the entrepreneur one of two vital advantages. It gives him either the ability to build a totally new kind of mousetrap, or the ability to build the old mousetrap in a new and better way. For example, the Boeing 747 jumbo jet was a successful new product because in 1970 no other plane could fly as many people as far; it was a totally new machine. Today the new European-built passenger jet called Airbus A-300 is on its way to becoming a commercial success because it is less expensive to buy and to operate than other planes of equal size and range; it does the same thing as its competitors, only better and more cheaply. Both the 747 and the Airbus A-300 are the products of technological innovations. Each, in its own unique way, is a better mousetrap.

Technological innovations are invariably the by-products of

23

basic scientific research. Somebody somewhere, working in a laboratory or hunched over a pile of books and charts, discovers something about the way our universe works which until that moment we had not understood. It may be something as basic as the laws of gravity or of electricity, or the fact that all living matter is composed of tiny cells. Or it may be the very composition of these cells; perhaps an insight into how they reproduce or how they fight infection. At first, of course, only the scientist is aware of his own discovery. Now he must begin to spread the word, so that others can understand what he has done and begin to make use of his new discovery in their own work. The scientist might spread the word by writing an article for some scientific journal, as Albert Einstein did in 1905 when he postulated his theory of relativity. Or he might spread the word by giving a lecture at some university, or perhaps at a conference of fellow scientists. The technique itself does not really matter. What matters is that the discovery becomes widely known and understood among experts in the field. In this way, it eventually becomes part of our general wealth of knowledge.

All of this takes time. It may be years or even decades before someone comes along who is able to develop a practical application for the original discovery. This will be the technological breakthrough that is the by-product of basic research; this will be the innovation that the entrepreneur will use to build his factory; to set the wheels turning that will create new jobs. For example, Einstein's theory of relativity was the basic scientific discovery. Laser technology was among the innovations that emerged, decades later, as a by-product of this discovery. Today corporations

24

throughout the U.S., Western Europe, and Japan manufacture and sell a wide variety of laser-related scientific and medical instruments, such as those CAT scanners that are used to detect cancerous tissues. These corporations are the entrepreneurs. They are the ones that made the huge financial investments required to put up factories—investments that in turn triggered the process of economic growth by creating new jobs for people to build the factories, to work in them, and to provide the goods and services that these new wage-earners were suddenly able to afford.

There is nothing new or radical about all this. We human beings have been making progress, more or less steadily, for a very long time. And when you look back across the centuries to see just how we have done it, you quickly realize that each step forward came through the process of economic growth, that each new level of growth was reached as the result of a technological innovation, and that each innovation was the by-product of a scientific discovery. For example, the science of agriculture began to develop in about the year 12,000 B.C., somewhere in what is now the Mideast. Centuries later, Roman agricultural scientists developed the "two-field" system of crop rotation; by keeping half the land fallow each year, the land becomes more fertile and so yield-per-acre increases. In the Middle Ages, European farmers replaced the "two-field" rotation system with the "three-field" system, and by doing so they increased yield-per-acre even more. Fields were now so fertile, in fact, that for the first time farmers were able to produce a crop of oats in the spring, as well as a crop in the autumn. The key technological innovation came in the eleventh century, when somebody whose name we do not know

25

invented the heavy-wheeled plow. Between the eleventh and thirteenth centuries, yield-per-acre doubled. Moreover, these plows were strong enough to clear forests when pulled by teams of horses—which farmers were now able to keep alive by feeding them spring oats. With so much new land available, farmers were able to raise enormous flocks of sheep. The wool from these sheep gave rise to a textile industry. This in turn created jobs for people to weave cloth, to sew it into clothing, and then to sell it.

As food and clothing became more abundant and therefore cheaper, standards of living began to rise sharply. Since people now had more purchasing power, they no longer had to build their own houses. This in turn created jobs for architects, engineers, carpenters, and other construction workers. Soon these workers were earning enough to support families of their own. The population began to grow more rapidly. And as it did demand increased for clothing, which in turn increased the number of jobs available in the textile industry. Trade among nations began to expand, and the need for commercial centers from which to conduct this trade gave rise to the development of cities. This in turn created jobs for people in banks, trading companies, and shops where city-dwellers could purchase products for their homes, such as food and furniture. In the eighteenth century, coal began to replace wood as a source of energy for heat. But coal could not be mined efficiently because most mines were full of water. In 1764 a Scottish chemist named Joseph Black, while studying the phenomenon of heat, discovered the relationships between heat, the boiling of water, and the resulting power of expanding steam. He explained all this to an engineer friend of his named

James Watt, who then designed the first practical steam engine.

The invention of the steam engine made possible the Industrial Revolution, and led to the creation of Western civilization as we know it today. The Revolution began in England, of course, where steam engines were used to pump water out of coal mines; this in turn enabled mine operators to increase production, which in turn enabled entrepreneurs to build factories that would use this coal for fuel. The Revolution spread to the United States in about 1790, when an English immigrant named Samuel Slater, who had learned how to build steam engines back in England, built an engine factory in Pawtucket, Rhode Island. Soon we Americans were making progress more rapidly than any other people in the world. In 1829, a scientist named Joseph Henry made important fundamental advances in the study of electricity. In 1834, Thomas Davenport built the first motor to be powered by electricity. In 1844, Samuel F. B. Morse perfected the electric telegraph. This device gave industry a fast, reliable communications system, which in turn helped trigger a sharp rise in the country's rate of economic growth. In 1839, Charles Goodyear discovered a process for vulcanizing rubber. And in 1859, Col. Edwin L. Drake drilled successfully for oil near Titusville, Pennsylvania. All of this, coupled with technological innovations such as Henry Ford's turn-of-the-century development of the modern assembly line, helped create the automobile industry; today this one industry is directly or indirectly responsible for more than one out of every ten jobs in the United States.

Our rate of progress during the twentieth century has been astounding. For example, scientific discoveries and technological innovations in agriculture have enabled us for the first time in history to produce as much food as we need. We even produce enough extra food to keep millions of people from starving to death who live in less progressive countries, such as India and the Soviet Union. And a steady drumbeat of discoveries and industrial innovations has led to the development of products that have improved our daily lives immeasurably—refrigerators, air conditioners, airplanes, synthetic fibers such as nylon and polyester, disposable diapers, life-saving wonder drugs such as penicillin. A complete list would fill a hundred pages. Even the shape of our culture has been profoundly changed by science and technology. We now have movies and television. And virtually every song that becomes a hit in the U.S. today is recorded with at least one musical instrument that did not exist thirty years ago, such as the electric guitar, the electronic piano, or the "Moog" synthesizer.

Clearly, entrepreneurs have always found the climate in our country to their liking. And as a result of their many successful efforts to manufacture and market the products of scientific discoveries and technological innovations, the U.S. economy during the twentieth century has expanded at a truly staggering rate. Today it is more than twice the size of any other economy in the world. This expansion has enabled the creation of more jobs, and more kinds of jobs, than have ever been created before in this or any other country. Moreover, literally millions of these jobs are in industries that did not even exist a few decades back, for example the electronic-equipment and computer industries. Our standard of living is the highest in the world, which means that there are more opportunities for more people in the U.S. to lead the kinds of lives they want, than are available to people in any other country. In short, we are history's most progressive civilization.

There is nothing mysterious about progress. We can hardly think of it as some dark, wondrous process that takes place now and then, here and there, for reasons that lie beyond our power to grasp. Progress is among the world's most visible, most glaringly obvious processes. We have made so much progress in our own country, and so much has been made in other countries as well, that we know more about progress than merely its components. We know what the process itself is like; we know its characteristics. We know what conditions enable progress to take place, and what conditions prevent it. We know what kinds of people we need to make progress, and we know what incentives they require to perform their functions. We know how to make progress take place rapidly, and we know how to slow it down. We know how to start up the process, and how to stop it dead in its tracks.

Progress is a complicated process. Under the best of circumstances it can take a long time for a discovery to become a job-creating product, and the path to success can be a very winding one indeed. For example, the word electricity was first coined by an English physician named Sir Thomas Browne in 1646. The incandescent bulb was invented by Thomas Edison in 1879. The first street was illuminated by electric power in New York in 1882. Literally since the Middle Ages, scientists have tried to duplicate the chemical reaction that occurs in fireflies and that produces "cold light." Only in 1971 was American Cyanamid Company able to market the Cyalume lightstick—a clear, wand-shaped plastic tube that throws off a yellow-green cold light.

Lightsticks are now used to monitor air pollution, and tests are under way to develop additional uses, from preventing food spoilage to making safer medicines.

Progress follows no set schedule, and it obeys no national borders. For instance, the idea of a mechanical digital computer was first conceived by an English mathematician named Charles Babbage in the 1830's. The first analog computer was built by an American engineer named Vannevar Bush in 1930. The first digital computer, caller Mark I, was constructed by a Harvard University professor named Howard Aiken in 1944. The first commercial computer was purchased by General Electric Company in 1954. And the first computers designed expressly for use by individuals in their own homes became available in 1977. No government agency could possibly have coordinated or directed all this. Bureaucrats simply do not see beyond tomorrow; they are not trained to see beyond tomorrow. A U.S. Commissioner of Patents named Henry L. Ellsworth once urged Congress to shut down the patent office on the grounds that there was nothing much left to invent. That was in 1844.

Progress is inevitably a risky, inconvenient process. No matter how careful scientists, engineers, and business executives may be— and most of these people are extremely careful indeed—things do sometimes go wrong. A drug reaches the market whose side effects are horrible. A new-fangled, highly-touted machine spews more pollution into the air, and makes more noise, than its designers had anticipated. A corporation makes one wrong move, goes bankrupt, and throws hundreds of employees out of work. None of these things should ever happen. But people make mistakes, so from time to time disasters occur; there is just no way to prevent them completely.

Even successful ventures contain an element of risk and inconvenience. Fifty years ago it was literally impossible to kill more than a dozen people in a single airplane accident. In 1977, when two jumbo jets collided on a fog-enshrouded runway in the Canary Islands, more than five hundred people lost their lives. And laboratories, power plants, factories, office buildings, shopping malls, housing tracts and the like all have to go somewhere. The amount of space available is limited. So we do sometimes encroach on our most attractive wilderness regions, we do sometimes turn farms into industrial parks and garden apartments, and we do sometimes disrupt old neighborhoods—all in the name of progress. But often this is what it takes to create jobs and to expand opportunities. Often there is just no other way to do it.

Progress is a very sensitive process. It slows down when governments interfere and try to manage it. Scientific research is most productive when scientists are left alone to follow their own judgments and instincts—to go where they want, to think about whatever interests them, to do whatever research they choose, to conduct whatever experiments they believe are necessary. New technologies are developed and deployed most rapidly and most efficiently when engineers are free to work and to tinker at their own speed, and in their own way. And economies grow most rapidly when entrepreneurs and other business executives are left alone by government agencies and bureaucrats; when the free market is allowed to decide who will fail and who will succeed. Indeed, the evidence to support this point is overwhelming. Today those countries whose people enjoy the most progress—whose people have the greatest opportunities to lead whatever sorts of lives they want—are those countries in which there is the most personal and industrial freedom, and the least government regulation and interference. More precisely, there is not a single socialist or communist country in which the standard of living is equal to the standard of living in even the smallest, least successful capitalist country. This can hardly be a coincidence.

Progress requires the accumulation of wealth. Unless some people have enough money to invest—unless some people are earning enough money so that they have some left over at the end of the month to put in the bank or in the stock market—entrepreneurs cannot obtain the huge sums of money they need to finance their ventures. And unless some people are earning enough money to buy the products that these entrepreneurs manufacture, their ventures obviously will go bankrupt. Moreover, progress is so very difficult to achieve that neither investors nor entrepreneurs will even make the effort unless they stand a chance of getting rich or richer from it. Naturally we celebrate the successful ventures and forget about the failures. But more often than not, attempts to turn ideas into discoveries, discoveries into innovations, and innovations into marketable products wind up in failure. More scientific experiments end with an unprintable curse than with an exultant cry of "Eureka!" More inventors die of broken hearts than of old age, and more entrepreneurs and investors lose money than make fortunes.

Progress is not for the lazy or the fainthearted. Whatever may be the outcome of a venture, the personal sacrifices required by the effort itself are staggering. Scientists work long hours in their laboratories. Engineers work equally hard in their workshops and their basements. It is a rare business executive who leaves his office promptly at five o'clock and who does not spend part of his weekend with a briefcase full of letters and reports that must be answered and read by Monday morning. Moreover, when other people depend utterly on your judgments and your success for their own jobs, the knowledge that you are responsible for the welfare of these people is a heavy burden to carry. In short, it takes a lot of hard work, risk, and emotional strain to actually make progress happen. The rewards of success must be substantial or no one will be willing to endure the hardships, the risks, and the emotional strains. And keep in mind that it is not only the people who make progress happen who benefit. Their successes create jobs for others. It seems odd at first, but the fact is that poor people escape from their poverty most rapidly in countries where there is a sufficient number of wealthy people to make the investments and the purchases that in turn create new jobs.

And finally, progress is an all-or-nothing kind of process. Expanded opportunities are the by-product of jobs. Jobs are the by-product of economic growth. Growth is the by-product of technological innovation. And technological innovation is the by-product of basic scientific research. The first cannot happen without the second, nor the second without the third, nor the third without the fourth, nor the fourth without the fifth. Each component must be in the right place, in the right position, at the right time. There is simply no such thing as progress without growth, or without technology, or without science—just as there is no such thing as a four-story building that has thirty feet of air where one of the stories ought to be. Remove any one component and the whole thing collapses. Yet today in the United States, and increasingly in other countries as well, the components of progress are under steady and sustained attack. It is this series of overt and covert attacks on economic growth, on technological innovation, and on basic scientific research that comprises the war against progress.

3

The Overt War

CHAPTER THREE

The first half of this war is made up of unconnected, self-contained battles—literally dozens of them—over specific projects in specific places. All of these battles are highly visible; indeed, we read about them in the papers nearly every day. In each case, the project under attack is one whose completion would either trigger economic growth, deploy a new technology, or lead to a basic discovery in one or another branch of science. Of course, in each case the enemies of progress insist that stopping progress is the furthest thing from their minds; they always offer a much more plausible justification for their attack. To be sure, none of these local battles is especially dangerous by itself. But all of them together pack a wallop whose impact on the country can be fatal, much in the way that a thousand tiny cuts can cause a man to bleed to death.

Of all the separate battles to stop progress by preventing economic growth, the fiercest is the one now raging in Alaska. At issue is whether or not to develop about one-third of this huge, resource-rich state. Environmentalists are fighting to prevent development, and their allies include the President of the United States, the Secretary of the Interior, and an overwhelming majority of the House of Representatives. President Carter has called the fight to prevent development of Alaska his Administration's "top environmental priority," and in May 1979 an anti-development bill supported by his Secretary of the Interior, Cecil Andrus, cleared the House of Representatives by a vote of 268 to 157. The bill would set aside 125 million acres of Alaskan territory. In doing so it would double the country's total park system by creating ten new parks and by enlarging three parks that already exist. Moreover, the bill would convert portions of this 125-million-acre chunk of real estate into national forests, wildlife refuges, or wild and scenic rivers that would then be subject to varying restrictions on use. And the bill would designate 67 million acres of the total as "wilderness," a special category that prohibits all permanent structures, all commercial enterprises, all roads, and all motor vehicles including airplanes.

This anti-growth bill will go a long way towards crippling the U.S. economy. For example, according to the U.S. Geological Survey there may be billions of barrels of undiscovered oil on land that would be "locked up" forever in the Arctic National Wildlife Refuge. The land may also contain trillions of cubic feet of natural gas. Moreover, mining companies report that they have already discovered a multi-billion-dollar deposit of copper, lead, zinc, and silver that extends into the proposed Gates of the Arctic National Wilderness in the western Brooks Range. Without new domestic supplies of vital materials such as copper, lead, zinc, and silver, the cost of all products containing these minerals will rise sharply as supplies grow scarce. This by itself will throw our economy into a tailspin. And our need for Alaska's oil and natural gas is almost too obvious to mention. Unless we can develop new domestic supplies of these fuels, our dependence on ultra-expensive foreign supplies will increase. If we buy the foreign fuel, its rising cost will drive our economy toward the breaking point. If we do not buy foreign fuel because we are unwilling or unable to pay the exorbitant prices set by those who have it to sell, our economy will skid to a halt for lack of energy. Indeed, this skid may already have begun. Within one week of the House of Representatives' vote, Americans once again were lining up at 5 a.m. for gasoline. Incredibly, not a single one of our country's major newspapers or television news programs pointed out the connection between these two events.

Even more than minerals and fuel, we need the jobs. Development of Alaska's energy and mineral resources would create thousands of jobs for unemployed Americans—building roads, building oil and gas pipelines, building and working in mines, building the heavy equipment for all these construction projects, building houses for the workers, running schools, hospitals, shops, movie theaters, restaurants, bowling alleys, and heaven knows what else for the workers and their families. Since Alaska's present population lives on less than 1 percent of the state's territory, there is plenty of room for careful, responsible development of a kind that would provide resources and create jobs without also ravaging the entire state. To the environmentalists and their allies, however, people apparently are less important than caribou, grizzly bears, walruses, and sea lions. For the environmentalists and their allies are not fighting to insure that as the land is developed, a portion of it will be set aside as a wilderness region. That would be a proper and eminently sensible thing to do. In fact, the territory that the environmentalists and their allies are fighting to withhold from development covers an area larger than the entire State of California.

Another fierce battle to stop progress by preventing economic growth is currently raging in Denver, Colorado. For more than five years now, environmentalists and their allies in the Federal government have successfully blocked the Foothills water project. This project, which was approved by the city's voters in a 1973 referendum, includes a 243-foot-high dam to be built on the South Platte River, a water treatment plant, and a reservoir. Its purpose is to double Denver's water supply, and by doing so to make it possible for more people to live and work in the region. Denver's need for more water is fairly pressing; since 1970 the population in the seven-county metropolitan area has increased by a whopping 28 percent. Moreover, it's likely that in the coming decade many more people will want or need to move to Denver. According to the U.S. Department of Energy, 55 percent of the country's coal reserves, 90 percent of its uranium ore, and 97 percent of its shale oil lie under the Western mountain states. As our country's need for these resources grows, Denver is certain to become an important center for oil, gas, and mineral exploration. Indeed, since 1974 the number of oil and gas exploration companies in Denver has just about tripled, from 350 to more than 1,000.

Environmentalists and their allies originally based their opposition to the Foothills water project on the grounds that Denver is already too large, and its air already too polluted, for the city's own good. Any further increase in the population, they argued, would be intolerable. Lately, opponents of the Foothills project have found a second justification for their battle to keep Denver from expanding. They have discovered that construction of the dam would flood a 96-acre chunk of open land, and by doing so would wipe out a rare species of butterfly. According to the Denver Water Board, even if the Foothills project goes forward now the opposition to it will have cost local taxpayers a fortune. When the project was first approved in that 1973 referendum, its cost was estimated at $65 million. Today, thanks largely to inflation, its cost is estimated at $135 million. How much the Foothills project will cost when it finally does begin—if it finally does begin —is difficult to estimate. In May 1978, the U.S. Environmental Protection Agency recommended to the Army Corps of Engineers that the permits necessary for construction be denied.

As their fight against economic growth has escalated, the enemies of progress have begun to deploy an especially nasty weapon. It is the imposition of arbitrary, artificial limits to the number of new homes and apartment units that may be built in a particular city or town. When you slap a limit on housing construction, you immediately deny jobs to architects, bricklayers, carpenters, electricians, and plumbers. You also reduce the number of jobs available for people who work in industries and businesses that manufacture and sell products for new houses and apartments, such as lumber, pipe, heating systems, washing machines, bathroom fixtures, and kitchen appliances. In the long run, a limit on housing construction even reduces the number of jobs available for people who work in businesses that manufacture and sell products mostly to people who have just purchased new homes or rented new apartments—lawnmowers, dishwashers, furniture, carpeting, curtains, and so forth. Moreover, when you slap a limit on housing construction in a particular city or town, you make it virtually impossible for economic growth to take place in that city or town. A company can not possibly expand an existing plant, or build a new one, if the workers who would arrive to claim the newly-created jobs will be unable to find places to live.

It is the devastating effect of housing-construction limits on our country's minority groups, such as our Black and Spanish-American citizens, that makes these limits so downright nasty. Obviously, many members of our minority groups are poor. And just as obviously, these people will not become comfortable or perhaps even affluent unless they can find jobs. But housing-construction limits inevitably reduce employment in precisely those businesses and industries—the building trades, for example—that offer the best job opportunities for people without college degrees and even for people without high school diplomas. Moreover, housing-construction limits make it impossible for people who live in our country's worst urban slums—that is, for minority-group Americans—ever to move out even if they do manage to find jobs. There is just nowhere for them to go. People who already own homes or rent apartments in our better cities, towns, and neighborhoods certainly cannot move out themselves just to make room; they also need places to live. So where are the new job-holders supposed to go once they can afford to leave their slum tenements? The answer, alas, is nowhere.

It is not a question of political or social theory. It is not even a question of economics. Rather, it is a matter of common sense. We can pass all the civil-rights laws and enact all the constitutional amendments we want. But unless we also build new houses and apartment units in our better cities, towns, and neighborhoods—in other words, unless we shove over to make room for more people on the higher rungs of the ladder, just as others once made room for us—we will never wipe out poverty among our country's minority-group citizens. Instead, we will insure that these people remain trapped where they are, in urban slums that are safely distant from our own comfortable neighborhoods. It is hardly an exaggeration to say that the most vicious racists in this country today are not those red-necked loudmouths who do the talking, but rather those politicians, bureaucrats, and social activists who struggle quietly to impose artificial limits on the number of new houses and apartment units that may be built in our cities, towns, and non-slum neighborhoods.

This particular weapon in the war against progress has been deployed most frequently in California. In 1972, residents of Petaluma, which is about forty miles north of San Francisco, voted to halt the physical growth of their lovely and prosperous city by setting rigid quotas on home construction. In March 1977, residents of Santa Barbara, a beautiful and extremely affluent city not far from Los Angeles, voted to do the same thing. And in November 1978, voters in San Jose re-elected with a plurality of more than 70 percent a mayor whose campaign had focused on a single issue—to control growth by restricting the number and location of new housing units; at the same time, San Jose's voters

43

tossed out of office a long-time member of the City Council who campaigned in support of unrestricted growth. In each of these California cities, the advocates of housing-construction limits argued that such measures were necessary to preserve and to protect the quality of life. To be sure, the lives whose quality they were preserving and protecting were their own. And the word they used most often to describe the drastic measure they were advocating was "progressive."

The use of housing-construction limits as a weapon for stopping economic growth has begun to spread eastward. In September 1977, voters in Boulder, Colorado, approved an ordinance that limits to 415 the number of new housing units that may be built each year. This artificial ceiling forces a 50 percent cut in the level of construction activity in one of our country's loveliest, most prosperous university towns. And in New York City's most prestigious and influential newspaper, *The New York Times*, articles and editorials have been published which suggest that the Big Apple has grown too big for its own good health; that to restore the city as an attractive place to live its current population must be made to shrink. The program proposed to trigger this shrinkage is the setting of limits on the construction of new housing. Appallingly but not surprisingly, these anti-growth articles and editorials were published at a time when unemployment in New York State—and in particular unemployment in the state's construction industry—was at a record high level.

In some parts of our country, campaigns are being fought to stop economic growth by discouraging, rather than actually preventing, any increase in the population. For example, in Oregon the former governor, Tom McCall, has launched what has come to be known as the visit-but-don't-stay movement. The objective of those who belong to this unabashedly inhospitable movement is to increase the number of tourists who visit Oregon each year— and who spend money there—while at the same time to bring about a decrease in the number of Americans who each year are moving permanently to Oregon. A similar movement has been under way for nearly a decade now in neighboring Washington. Indeed, a columnist for *The Seattle Post-Intelligencer* named Emmett Watson urges readers to "fight 'em off, do your part," by warning out-of-state friends and relatives who might be thinking of resettling in Washington of the region's persistent, "keep-'em-away rain." And in Hawaii, anti-growth partisans are campaigning not only to hold down the state's permanent population, but even to clamp a limit on the number of tourists who will come to visit. More precisely, these partisans are opposing the construction of new hotels and resorts. Since tourism is Hawaii's largest and most job-creating industry, success in this campaign would deal a devastating economic blow to many of that state's present residents.

Battles to delay or permanently halt the construction of new facilities for generating power have become a major feature of the war against progress. And no wonder. A country's economy cannot possibly grow without an adequate supply of energy. For there is not a single product which can be manufactured without the use of at least some energy somewhere in the production process. Introduce a new product, or increase production of an existing product, and the need for energy inevitably expands. Hire more people to develop products, and then to sell and service these products, and you also need more energy; scientists, engineers, and office employees obviously cannot work in the dark or in the cold. Indeed, it is even impossible for an individual businessman or businesswoman to operate a small, "non-polluting" business without at least some energy. For instance, it is hard to imagine a business that is less industrialized, and that adds less pollution to our atmosphere, than raising flowers in a commercial hothouse. But those flowers must be kept alive by energy-consuming heaters and humidifiers. And the owner of any kind of shop will tell you that customers would not linger over merchandise if they are shivering from a lack of heat, or squinting for a lack of light.

Simply put, then, factories and other businesses are able to survive and expand—and by doing so to create jobs—only when enough energy is available to provide however much fuel may be needed to keep things running smoothly. This is a fact of economic life. It applies to all countries and all economic systems. There is no way around it. Among other things, this fact means that the directors of large corporations will never vote to invest billions or even millions of dollars in new factories, new research laboratories, or new office facilities unless they are reasonably certain that in the years to come there will be enough energy available to keep the new operation humming. It also means that individual business-men and women will not launch new businesses, or expand old ones, in regions where energy supplies are scarce and future supplies uncertain. Delay or permanently halt the construction of energy-generating facilities, then, and you guarantee a lack of economic growth and therefore a lack of new jobs. You prevent opportunities from expanding. You stop progress dead in its tracks.

Battles to limit the supply of energy have been fought from one end of this country to the other. For example, enemies of progress have stopped the Tennessee Valley Authority from completing its $116 million hydroelectric project on the Little Tennessee River. They have derailed the $700 million Dickey-Lincoln hydroelectric project on Maine's Upper St. John River. They have driven the cost of the Kaiparowits coal-fired electric power plant in Utah to such a prohibitive level—up sevenfold, from the original estimate of $500 million to a current estimate of $3.5 billion—that the consortium of utility companies that had planned to build the plant no longer can afford to do so. And for more than twelve years now, enemies of progress have kept the Consolidated Edison Company of New York from completing a pumped-storage facility near Cornwall, New York. More than a dozen other power facilities around the U.S. have never even moved off the drawing boards, because opponents of these proposed projects have successfully kept the utility companies involved from purchasing the necessary land.

This struggle to stop the construction of power projects has been matched by an equally determined struggle to limit our supply of oil. For nearly a decade, enemies of progress managed to prevent all exploration-drilling projects off the East coast, in Baltimore Canyon. At the same time, they have effectively stopped all drilling operations off the coast of California. And to make sure we cannot meet our rising energy needs by importing oil, they have steadfastly fought to block construction of deep-water ports that would be large enough to handle today's super-tankers.

Opponents of new energy projects have been extremely careful never to suggest that their battles, if successful, would stop

47

economic growth and therefore prevent the creation of new jobs. The court injunction they won to stop the Tennessee Valley Authority project was based on the grounds that if the project were completed, it would doom a little fish called the Tennessee snail darter. Their opposition to the Dickey-Lincoln facility rests on the claim that completion of this project would threaten a local plant called the Furbish lousewort. And their opposition to the Kaiparowits coal-fired electric power plant in Utah is based on the claim that completion of this project would endanger the health and safety of certain local residents. The local residents cited are the kangaroo rat and the black-footed ferret.

Today's far-reaching campaign to stop the deployment of new technologies is yet another feature of the overt war against progress. Indeed, this campaign has been an especially destructive part of the overall struggle. Throughout history new technologies have always led to new products, which in turn have led to economic growth and to the creation of new jobs. But the link between technology and growth has traditionally been stronger in the United States than in any other country. According to a report made public in 1977 by the U.S. Department of Commerce, technological innovations were directly responsible for 45 percent of our country's economic growth between 1929 and 1969. The Commerce Department study also compared the performances of technology-intensive corporations with the performances of all other corporations between 1957 and 1973; it found that the technology-intensive corporations created new jobs 88 percent faster than the others. It is hardly surprising, then, that the enemies of progress have campaigned with such grim determination to stop the vital process of technological innovation.

The first successful battle to prevent the deployment of a new technology was fought in Washington, D.C. in December 1970. That was when the United States Senate, by a vote of 52 to 41, rejected a request by the Nixon Administration for $290 million to help finance development of an American supersonic transport airplane. The immediate impact of this vote was to eliminate 4,800 jobs for aircraft workers who had been designing and building SST prototypes. The long-range impact of the vote has been considerably more destructive. Back in December 1970, the U.S. was the world leader in commercial aircraft sales. By turning this country's back on the SST, however, the Senate gave foreign aircraft manufacturers a remarkable chance to increase their tiny shares of the growing world market—at the direct expense of U.S. manufacturers, and of course at the expense of U.S. workers.

Not surprisingly, foreign aircraft manufacturers moved swiftly to take advantage of their opportunity. Today the only supersonic transport jet in regular commercial service is the *Concorde*, which is built by companies in Great Britain and France. Construction and deployment of the *Concorde* has created thousands of jobs for aircraft and airline workers in those countries. Moreover, the West Europeans have begun to use the technological skills they developed by manufacturing the world's first SST to build first-rate subsonic commercial airplanes, such as the European Airbus. So efficient is this particular jet that our own Eastern Airlines recently announced plans to buy at least twenty of them. This decision marked the first time in U.S. aviation history that a domestic airline bought planes that were manufactured by a foreign company, and built by foreign workers. Moreover, many non-U.S. airlines whose passenger fleets had been made up exclusively of American-built jet planes have now begun to purchase European Airbus jets. Indeed, in March 1979 the company that manufactures these planes, Airbus Industrie, announced that to meet rising demand production will be tripled and then quadrupled —an expansion that will increase the number of jobs in the European aircraft industry from 17,000 to more than 40,000. The victims of this remarkable expansion will be U.S. aircraft manufacturers and, of course, American aircraft workers who will either lose their jobs or be unable to find jobs in this country.

As always, the enemies of progress were careful not to link their opposition to the SST with the notion of progress. They based their successful fight to keep the U.S. from building this plane on two arguments: that the SST might conceivably cause skin cancer by hampering formation of the ozone layer of our atmosphere, which filters out ultraviolet light, and that the plane would create intolerable noise at airports. The first argument was subsequently dismissed by scientists, and the second argument was totally discredited by the results of noise-level tests performed over lengthy periods of time at airports both in Washington, D.C. and New York. Indeed, the *Concorde* turned out to be quieter than certain older, subsonic airplanes that have been in regular commercial service for years. But the battle in 1970 to stop deployment of an American-built SST was more than merely an error of scientific judgment. Rather, it was the first time in our country's history that we made a conscious decision to surrender the lead in any technology whatsoever. That the specific technological lead we chose to surrender was in the field of aerospace is especially noteworthy. Just seventeen months prior to that Senate vote, the United States landed the first men on the moon.

Today the most ferocious battles to stop technological innovation are those being fought against nuclear power. Like any new technology, this one is imperfect and therefore inherently risky. Just how imperfect and just how risky is very much a matter of how you look at it. On the one hand, in more than two decades of nuclear power generation in the U.S., not a single member of the public has been killed or injured in any accident of any sort whatever. On the other hand, in the aftermath of Three Mile Island even the most ardent advocates of nuclear power have come to recognize that improvements must be made in our nuclear reactor equipment and in our procedures for licensing and operating nuclear power plants. Nevertheless, just two weeks after the accident at Three Mile Island—an event that scared us half to death but that in fact took no lives and caused no injuries—a Gallop Poll showed that the majority of Americans continues to support nuclear power.

But if the enemies of progress have their way, nuclear power will be stopped forever in the U.S.—despite continuing public support for it, and no matter how safe we may be able to make our equipment and procedures. For instance, they have introduced propositions to ban nuclear power permanently in seven states— Arizona, California, Colorado, Montana, Ohio, Oregon, and Washington. In three states—Montana, South Dakota, and Vermont—they have campaigned successfully for laws that either ban the siting of nuclear waste repositories or that impose virtually insurmountable obstacles to siting waste repositories on their territories; they are lobbying for similar legislation in a half-dozen other states. In Missouri they have rammed through the state legislature a bill that forbids utilities from passing on to customers the costs of building nuclear power plants until those plants are actually operating. This measure, which makes it extremely difficult for utilities to raise enough money for expansion, effectively prevents the construction of ultra-expensive nuclear power plants anywhere in the state. In New Hampshire, enemies of progress have delayed for more than twelve years completion of a nuclear plant at Seabrook. In Vermont, they have campaigned successfully in thirty-three communities for referendums that ban construction of nuclear power plants. In New Jersey they have managed to delay and perhaps to permanently destroy plans by the Public Service Electric and Gas Company to build a $2.1 billion nuclear generating station in the ocean, about twelve miles northeast of Atlantic City. And across the U.S. they are demonstrating and lobbying to shut down as many operating nuclear power plants as possible.

This campaign to permanently stop nuclear power would not be so threatening—so very dangerous—were it a thing apart. But in fact it is merely one key battle in the larger effort to inhibit economic growth by holding down the supply of energy. It is important to keep in mind that our need for nuclear power has developed so rapidly during the last twenty years because during this period we have begun to run short of oil; if we had more oil to fuel conventional power plants, nuclear power plants would not be so vitally important. Now it happens that our problem is not simply a shortage of crude oil, but also a shortage of refined oil that can be used as fuel. In other words, we do not have a sufficient number of refineries. Why not? Because of the twenty-three large refineries that various oil companies have proposed in the last twenty years, twenty-one have been abandoned in the face of public protests or rejected outright by local zoning boards, state regulators or the federal government itself. In a very real sense, the people who today are fighting so desperately to stop nuclear power are the same people who have made us so dependent on it in the first place.

The fight against basic scientific research has won fewer headlines than the fight against technological innovation. But in a way, the campaign that is now raging in the U.S. to stop the advance of science is the most ominous part of the overt war against progress. For if today's technologies are to be rejected for one reason or another—because they are too dangerous, because they are too expensive, because they threaten certain endangered species of animal or plant—then our only hope for making progress is to develop new technologies that will be better than the ones presently at our disposal.

But new technologies do not appear on command, or at the touch of a button on someone's computer. They appear infrequently, and even then only as the by-products of basic scientific research. Inhibit scientific research, then, and the chances become very slim indeed for making any progress at all in the years and decades to come. And this is precisely what the enemies of progress are attempting to do. Not content merely to stop deployment of today's admittedly imperfect technologies, they are fighting as well to destroy the only process that is capable of producing more perfect technologies for tomorrow.

One key target in the battle against science has been a promising branch of biology called gene-splicing. More formally known as recombinant DNA research, gene-splicing involves the separation and then "re-combination" of DNA—deoxyribonucleic acid —which is the active substance in the genes of all living things. DNA governs the heredity of life itself; it is the chemical that enables us to pass on to our offspring our physical and mental characteristics. At least in theory, it might be possible to "special order" the characteristics of an offspring by splicing together the parents' genes in a way that wouldn't happen naturally. The point of doing such a thing would be to eliminate an undesirable trait, such as a tendency towards certain hereditary diseases, or to replace an undesirable trait with one that is more desirable.

At the moment, gene-splicing is more an idea than a practical technique. Indeed, it was not until July 1978 that a group of scientists from Harvard University, Yale University, and Turkey's Hacettepe University succeeded in identifying, for the first time, a single gene from among the millions in one human cell. But scientists believe that should they ever master the process of gene-splicing, its potential applications would be incredibly diverse —and extraordinarily valuable. For example, scientists believe that gene-splicing could vastly increase the world's food supply by enabling the manufacture of vaccines to prevent swine and cattle diseases, and by enabling plant genes to manufacture their own nitrogen fertilizer from the air. They believe that gene-splicing could provide the key to development of chemical compounds that would help clean up oil spills. It could also make possible the manufacture of new drugs, such as synthetic insulin for diabetics. And some scientists believe that one day, perhaps within our life-times, the use of "gene therapy" will make it possible to wipe out hereditary diseases, such as sickle cell anemia.

Despite the potential benefits of gene-splicing, the enemies of progress have fought to frustrate the efforts of U.S. scientists to learn more about this complex process. For example, in 1976 the city council of Cambridge, Massachusetts, voted to halt all gene-splicing experiments at two of this country's most distinguished and responsible scientific installations, both of which just happen to be located within the Cambridge city limits. One of these installations belongs to Harvard University, and the other to the Massachusetts Institute of Technology. Since that vote, similar measures in other communities to either restrict or ban gene-splicing experiments have been called for by more than a dozen major U.S. newspapers and political leaders. In 1977, following a recommendation by high-level officials in eight federal agencies, the U.S. Congress began to consider a number of proposed bills to establish national regulations for the conduct of DNA research. In one way or another, each of the proposed bills restricted the freedom of our country's biologists to conduct their research. And in December 1978, the Department of Health, Education, and Welfare issued a set of "guidelines" for the conduct of gene-splicing research that prohibits all U.S. scientists—those working for the government, those working for universities, those working for industry—from conducting six entire categories of experiments.

Biology is not the only branch of science that has come under fire from the enemies of progress. Attacks have also been launched against selected branches of oceanography, geology, chemistry, and physics. For example, the City of New York has been fighting for nearly ten years now to keep Columbia University, which is located in Manhattan, from conducting any experiments whatever with its 250-kilowatt, Triga Mark II nuclear reactor. The machine itself, which would be used primarily for teaching, was completed in 1969. It has not yet been allowed to operate. Indeed, it may never operate; in April 1979 the president of Columbia University, bowing to student pressure, forced the engineering faculty to accept an unlimited moratorium on use of the reactor. And all branches of scientific research made a narrow escape back in 1975, when the House of Representatives actually passed a bill that would have required Congressional clearance for each and every research grant approved by the National Science Foundation. Fortunately, this bill died in the Senate.

As always, the enemies of progress have been careful never to suggest that their efforts to undermine science are part of a larger effort to inhibit progress itself. They have invariably emphasized their own enthusiasm and support for progress, and they have always found a plausible explanation on which to pin their opposition to any one specific project. For example, the Congressman who introduced that bill requiring all National Science Foundation grants to be approved in advance by members of Congress said his only purpose was to make sure that none of the public's money would be wasted on projects that were impractical. Yet not a single member of Congress, at least then, was a trained scientist. The City of New York says its opposition to the use of a nuclear reactor by Columbia University is based on the fear that once operating, the reactor would be a target for "urban terrorists." Yet according to qualified scientists, the most destructive thing a terrorist could threaten to do with a reactor of this type would be to pick up and throw it at somebody. And the mayor of Cambridge, Massachusetts, cited public safety as his primary motive for voting to stop gene-splicing experiments at the Harvard and M.I.T. laboratories. "Something could crawl out of the laboratory, such as Frankenstein," he explained to reporters. Scientists say that's ridiculous.

This, then, is the overt portion of the war against progress. This is what it looks like; this is the shape of it. It is a series of separate, unconnected battles to either slow down or permanently stop specific projects in specific places around the country. In each instance, the project under attack would expand opportunities for Americans by creating jobs for them. It would do this either by stimulating economic growth directly, or by stimulating growth indirectly through the deployment of a new technology or through a discovery in some branch of scientific research. Again, it is important to keep in mind that none of these battles is especially dangerous by itself. The United States is hardly a small or a delicate country, vulnerable to destruction from the slightest blow. We are a large and powerful country, and we can absorb an enormous amount of punishment. Our fate will never rest on the outcome of any one battle to stop progress. But not even the U.S. could survive the loss of too many of these battles. And today the enemies of progress are chalking up more wins than losses. Moreover, their successes on the battlefield have been enhanced by even greater successes behind the lines. That is, their clandestine, covert campaign to stop progress has already brought them a long way toward final victory. Indeed, it may well turn out to be this latter effort which decides the outcome of the war.

CHAPTER

4

The Covert War

CHAPTER FOUR

The covert half of this war is a campaign to stop progress by destroying the economic power of those who make progress happen. That is, by preventing those who earn money from keeping it to do with as they please. After all, money is the fuel of progress. A country's economy simply cannot run without it. People need money to buy the goods and services that make possible a comfortable or merely decent standard of living. Entrepreneurs need money to build their factories, and by doing so to turn new technologies into marketable products. And established corporations need money to train scientists and engineers, to supply them with equipment, to finance the huge research-and-development programs that produce new technologies, and of course to build whatever new facilities are necessary to provide the various products that corporations are in business to manufacture and sell.

These are the activities that create jobs, and all of them cost money. Lots of it. The more money that remains in people's pockets—to spend, to save, and most importantly to invest in fledgling companies and established corporations—the more new jobs a country can create and therefore the more progress it can make. And the more money that is siphoned out of people's pockets —and the less the remaining money is worth—the fewer jobs a country can create and therefore the harder it becomes for that country to make any progress at all. Siphon out too much money, or force down its value too far, and eventually a country's economic engines will burn themselves out.

For several years now, the enemies of progress have been working to siphon out money from the pockets of those who earn it. They have been doing this in much the same way as petty thieves who siphon out gasoline from parked cars on a street. Indeed, the similarities are fairly striking. For instance, petty thieves are always careful never to drain any one tank completely dry, and by doing so to alert their victims. Moderation and repetition are the keys to their success. The dollar loss of each "hit" must be low enough so that the victims will not bother to call in the police or, worse for the thieves, put gasoline beyond their reach by parking in locked garages. So the gasoline thieves swipe a pint from this car, a quart from that one, a half-gallon from the Chevrolet across the street and a gallon from the Ford pick-up down the block. As the number of "hits" climbs, the total take becomes enormous. And this is precisely how the enemies of progress go about their business. They siphon out a dollar here, ten dollars there, a hundred dollars from this victim and a thousand or perhaps a million from that one.

If you ask what lies behind this present frenzy in our country to soak the rich, and even to soak the moderately comfortable among us, the enemies of progress will tell you their objective is equality. And it is—but not the kind of equality we are used to in the U.S. For they do not want equality of opportunity. Not at all. They want equality of condition. And they mean to get it by steadily transferring wealth from those who have it to those who do not. Put another way, the enemies of progress want to level out the economic peaks and valleys in our country by lopping off the peaks and using what's removed to build up the valleys.

For as they see it, there is something terribly wrong with an economic system that allows some people to have more wealth than other people. A wide range of wealth is unfair; it is intolerable. Moreover, they tell us, we are entering a new era of economic limits. The pie can no longer continue to grow. And since some of us right now do not have adequate slices, so to speak, those whose slices are bigger than absolutely necessary to get along—those who are comfortable or affluent, in other words—will have to surrender a portion to those who need it. In an era of limits, survival means sharing; and sharing means preventing the accumulation of wealth —by siphoning out money from the pockets of those who have it and then transferring this money to those whose pockets are empty.

Taxation has far and away been the most effective technique for siphoning out money from people's pockets. Between 1946 and 1976, the amount of money removed annually through taxation increased elevenfold, from $52 billion to $590 billion. Yet during this same period there was only an eightfold increase in our gross national product (G.N.P.), which is the total dollar value of all goods and services produced and provided in any one year. In other words, during this thirty-year period the government took out of our pockets a larger and larger percentage of the money that we were able to earn; each year we were left with a smaller and smaller percentage of the money we had earned to invest or to spend on whatever goods and services we wanted. And of course, since 1976 the situation has continued to deteriorate. For example, in 1978 taxation removed an estimated $656 billion from the economy. This figure equals 41 percent of our total national income. Some economists have lately calculated that if the present tax trends continue, by the year 2000 government will be taking fifty cents of every dollar earned.

Contrary to popular belief it is the rich and the moderately comfortable—not the indigent and the working poor—who have been shouldering the burden of rising tax rates. According to the Treasury Department, 50 percent of all families in the U.S. have incomes of at least $10,000 a year. And according to the Internal Revenue Service, in 1976 these families paid 94 percent of all taxes collected. That means families with incomes of less than $10,000 in 1976 paid just 6 percent of all taxes collected. And the rich and the moderately affluent among us have actually been shouldering more of the burden with each passing year. For example, the wealthiest 25 percent of taxpayers in the U.S.—those with incomes of at least $17,000—paid 68 percent of all taxes collected in 1970; in 1975 they paid 72 percent of all taxes collected and in 1976 they paid 75 percent. By contrast, the bottom 50 percent of taxpayers—those earning less than $10,000—paid 10 percent of all taxes collected in 1970, 7 percent in 1975 and just 6 percent in 1976.

The campaign to transfer wealth has been the single most

important cause of this steady rise in taxes. For example, in 1977 transfer payments by the federal government totaled more than $250 billion. In fact this was the single largest expenditure in the federal budget—larger even than our expenditure on defense. According to figures published by the U.S. Treasury Department, and by the Institute for Socioeconomic Studies, the percentage of our country's national income that goes for transfer payments has nearly tripled in the last fifteen years, from 6.5 percent in the early 1960's to 19 percent in 1977. Moreover, in 1977 the money appropriated for transfer programs came to 70 percent of all federal tax receipts.

Government borrowing is another technique the enemies of progress have utilized to transfer wealth. Between 1946 and 1976, that elevenfold increase in taxation was matched by a thirteenfold increase in total government expenditures. In other words our local governments, our state governments, and especially the federal government have been spending money faster than they have been collecting it. And to cover their deficits, which in 1976 alone totaled $44 billion, these governments have been doing precisely what people do when they plunge into debt. That is, our governments have been borrowing heavily from individuals and institutions, such as banks and pension funds, that have money available to lend. Normally, these individuals and institutions would loan their money to entrepreneurs and businesses, for instance by buying shares of stock issued by fledgling companies and by established corporations. To entice investors away from these job-creating borrowers, the various governments have been issuing bonds, treasury notes, and other securities that are more attractive than any securities the entrepreneurs and corporations are able to offer. For example, government securities are generally less risky than corporate securities because governments tend not to go bankrupt. And government securities are tax-exempt, which of course makes them especially attractive to investors. All too often, the advantages of government securities have proved too great to ignore. As a result, our governments have been able to siphon out of the marketplace an enormous amount of money—money that otherwise would have been available to entrepreneurs and to large corporations to finance growth, technological innovation, and scientific research. In just the last five years, funds raised under the auspices of just the federal government have ranged from 25 percent to 40 percent of all borrowing in the U.S. economy.

Regulation has become a third technique to transfer wealth. Between 1951 and 1978, the number of bureaucrats employed by the federal government to regulate business increased from 20,000 to 130,000. The number of regulatory agencies more than doubled, leaping from twenty to forty-one. No one has been able to calculate just how many new regulations have been promulgated during this period. However, the Commission on Federal Paperwork now estimates that government regulators crank out enough documents each year—each year—to fill fifty-one major-league baseball stadiums. To be sure, some of these documents are perfectly sensible and proper, such as those which outline safety standards for airplane landing gear. But other documents are simply impossible to justify because they are not only superfluous to the country's health and welfare but also utterly ridiculous. The Occupational Safety and Health Administration once issued an illustrated pamphlet that shows farmers how to avoid slipping on cow dung.

Today the cost of regulation is at a record level. For example, since 1974 the combined budget of the federal government's forty-one regulatory agencies has more than doubled, from $2.2 billion to $4.8 billion in fiscal 1979. This increase reflects a growth rate that exceeds the growth rate of the federal budget as a whole, the growth rate of the U.S. population, and the growth rate of the U.S. gross national product. More importantly, the costs of complying with federal government regulations have become astronomical. According to no less an authority than the White House, regulation takes $2,000 a year out of the pocket of the typical American family—a larger sum than is collected in federal taxes.

And the cost of regulation to corporations is even more appalling. This year, according to a report published by Washington University's Center for the Study of American Business, U.S. corporations will spend more than $100 billion to satisfy the requirements of federal regulations. In other words, regulation this year will siphon out from corporate treasuries more than $100 billion that would otherwise be available to invest in projects that would create new jobs—new research-and-development programs, programs to market products based on new technologies, programs to build new factories and offices for the people who would participate in these growth-related projects.

In addition to siphoning out huge sums of money from people's pockets, the enemies of progress have managed to lower the value of whatever money they have allowed us to keep. They have done this by expanding the supply of money at a faster rate than the

67

expansion of the economy itself. Money of course, is subject to the same economic laws as everything else. That is, the more units that exist the less each unit is worth. Print too many dollars, then, and the value of each dollar drops. And as the value of each dollar drops, the prices of all things that dollars purchase—in other words, all goods and all services—inevitably go up to compensate for the change. This is inflation. And in recent years, in their drive to increase government spending far beyond any level our economy could realistically support, the enemies of progress have kept the government's printing presses in high gear. Since 1960, the U.S. economy has grown by less than 90 percent. During this same period, the supply of money has exploded by nearly 380 percent. The result is today's virulent inflation—an affliction whose primary symptom is the sharp decline of opportunity.

Obviously it is a question of degree. Government is a vitally important institution, and no country can survive without one. Indeed, the only thing worse than Big Government is no government at all, since anarchy kills more people than repression. So it would be foolish to argue or to believe that all taxation is destructive, that all government borrowing is ruinous, that all regulation is superfluous, or that any expansion of the money supply is dangerous. But there is a line between necessary taxation and destructive taxation, a line between prudent government borrowing and ruinous borrowing, a line between sensible regulation and superfluous regulation, and a line between careful expansion of the money supply and dangerous expansion of it. The enemies of progress are fighting to drag our country across these lines. By imposing exorbitant tax rates, by plunging our governments more and more deeply into debt, and by strangling our most creative and productive individuals, universities, and corporations in the red tape of regulation, the enemies of progress have already siphoned out much of the fuel that our economic engines require to run efficiently and at high speed. And by expanding the money supply too rapidly, they have thrown the U.S. economy into an inflationary tailspin that makes genuine progress nearly impossible for most Americans to achieve no matter how hard they try.

This, then, is the covert portion of the war against progress. It is a combination of policies and programs that stop progress by destroying the economic power of those who make progress happen. Just as with the overt portion of the war, no one covert attack would be especially dangerous by itself. However, all of the attacks together have begun to have an absolutely devastating impact on our country. In fact, today we are moving forward more slowly than we have ever moved forward before. And the situation is deteriorating. There are ominous indications now that in the years to come, our country's rate of progress will be even lower than it is today.

For example, we are less productive than we used to be. Productivity, which is the average output per hour of labor, is one of the most accurate measures of a country's rate of progress. The higher a country's productivity rate, the more its workers are producing. And the more goods and services a country's workers produce, the more new jobs that are created and the more opportunities there are for people to lead whatever kinds of lives they want. Through all of the 1950's and most of the 1960's, productivity in the U.S. increased at an annual rate of nearly 3 percent.

However, between 1968 and 1976—a period that coincides almost precisely with the outbreak of the war against progress—productivity in the U.S. increased at an annual rate of only 1.5 percent. That's exactly half the earlier rate.

By early 1979, according to the U.S. Department of Labor, productivity in the U.S. was increasing at an annual rate of just 1.1 percent. That's almost nothing at all. This swift slide in the U.S. productivity growth rate is especially striking when the performances of other countries are measured against our own performance. Between 1967 and 1977, U.S. productivity in manufacturing increased a total of 27 percent. During the same period, productivity in manufacturing increased 107 percent in Japan, 72 percent in France, 70 percent in West Germany, 62 percent in Italy, and 43 percent in Canada. The only industrial country whose manufacturing productivity between 1967 and 1977 grew at the same rate as the U.S., 27 percent, is Great Britain—a country regularly cited by U.S. political leaders and commentators as an economic cripple whose fate we must be careful not to duplicate.

We are much less innovative than we used to be. Since new technologies are so vital to progress, the speed at which a country develops innovations is also a good measure of its rate of progress. And one of the best indicators of technological innovation is the balance of patents, which compares the number of patents granted to foreigners in the world's eleven most technologically advanced countries—the U.S., Belgium, Canada, Denmark, Great Britain, Ireland, Japan, Luxembourg, the Netherlands, the Soviet Union, and West Germany. According to the National Science Foundation, between 1966 and 1977 the U.S. patent balance fell by

47 percent. This staggering drop was due to a 91 percent increase in the number of patents granted to non-Americans during these years by the U.S. government, coupled with a leveling off and eventual decline in the number of patents granted to U.S. citizens during those years by foreign governments. Today the U.S. has a favorable but declining patent balance with Canada, Great Britain, and five West European countries. Our patent balances with West Germany and Japan are actually negative.

These numbers show that the U.S. has already begun to lose its once overwhelming technological lead. They show that other countries are swiftly closing the gap. Moreover, it is apparent from these numbers that some countries have actually begun to pull ahead of the U.S. in the all-important race for technological innovation. Indeed, we need hardly rely on statistics alone to know that we have in fact begun to falter. The evidence is visible all around us that today more than ever before in this century, major technological breakthroughs are being achieved in countries other than our own. The world's fastest commercial jet plane, the *Concorde*, is manufactured and sold by companies in Great Britain and France. (What matters is not so much the machine itself—which is imperfect, simply because it is the first version of a radically new design—but rather the experience and expertise acquired by the companies that built it. Even if rising fuel prices coupled with environmental opposition do force the *Concorde* to be grounded it will be the English and the French, not their U.S. competitors, who will eventually dominate the airplane-manufacturing industry by one day producing an improved, profitable SST.) One of the world's most efficient and popular subsonic

71

passenger jets, the European Airbus, is manufactured and sold by a French-West German consortium. The diesel engine was first available on foreign cars; so were front-wheel drive, disc brakes, and radial tires. The world's most advanced high-pressure injection moulding machinery, which is used to manufacture plastic products such as bottles, comes from West Germany. And today 100 percent of our television video-tape recorders are made in Japan.

It is not the injury to our national pride that is so devastating. Rather, it is the injury to our economic and even our social engines. New technologies are the catalysts of economic growth. And growth is the process—the one and only process—that creates new jobs and that by doing so expands opportunities. Because a growing percentage of the world's newest technologies are being developed and deployed outside the U.S., the economic growth that is made possible by these new technologies is taking place in countries other than our own. And the new jobs that are being created as the by-products of this growth are being created for foreign workers rather than for Americans. At the same time, the absence of new technologies in the U.S. is making economic growth in this country harder and harder to achieve. We struggle more to accomplish less, which is why our productivity growth rate has begun to plummet. Moreover, as the quality of our products declines relative to the quality of similar products manufactured in other countries, the market for our products inevitably declines as customers increasingly buy products manufactured by our foreign competitors. And as the market for U.S. products shrinks, so too does the number of new jobs our industries are able to create.

Our country's research and development efforts have begun to taper off. According to the National Science Foundation, total expenditures in the U.S. for research and development declined from 2.8 percent of our gross national product in 1968 to 2.25 percent of G.N.P. in 1976. During this same period, expenditures for basic research and development in Japan, West Germany, and even the Soviet Union all showed a marked increase when measured as a percentage of those countries' gross national products. Between 1968 and 1978, the number of scientists and engineers engaged in research in the U.S. dropped by 13 percent. During this same period, the number of scientists and engineers engaged in research went up by 55 percent in the Soviet Union, 59 percent in West Germany, and 62 percent in Japan. In 1967, according to a report issued recently by the U.S. government, 50 percent of the world's basic research and development was conducted in this country. However, the report added, in 1977 only 20 percent of the world's basic research and development was conducted in the U.S. The results of our earlier efforts were especially visible in 1976, when U.S. scientists made a clean sweep of the Nobel prizes. But if our expenditures for basic research and development continue to deteriorate—or even if they remain at today's low levels—this kind of awesome accomplishment will be impossible to duplicate in a decade's time.

The rising cost of regulation is now forcing our country's most creative and productive corporations to slash their research and development programs. For example, in 1977 E.I. Dupont de Nemours Company announced that it would close down its research laboratory in Old Hickory, Tennessee. It was at Old

Hickory that Dupont conducted some of the experiments that led to the development of synthetic fibers, such as Dacron and Orlon. These two fibers helped create a synthetic textile industry, which today provides jobs for thousands of Americans. Moreover, citing the excessive costs and regulation-related difficulties of conducting long-term research and development programs, Dupont recently announced that it would abandon twenty-two of what the company calls "new adventures." These are costly, high-risk research and development projects designed to produce major new discoveries and breakthroughs. Also in 1977, decisions to close down or curtail research laboratories were announced by Aluminum Company of America, Bethlehem Steel Corp., and Zenith Radio Corp. To be sure, other U.S. corporations have announced plans to maintain or even increase their expenditures for basic research and development. But more often than not, the additional money will be burned up for purposes other than the search for new discoveries and new technological innovations. General Motors Corp. has reported that 50 percent of the money it now spends for basic research and development is allocated exclusively to projects that are necessary to satisfy the requirements of government regulations.

Some kinds of research and development now are banned outright; other kinds we are abandoning voluntarily. In December 1977, a group of prominent scientists meeting in Bethesda, Maryland, was told that as a direct result of U.S. government restrictions on recombinant DNA research, certain key experiments in this promising branch of biology that were under way in Western Europe simply were off-limits to our own scientists.

And in August 1978, the Senate Appropriations Committee voted to delete from the National Aeronautics and Space Administration's budget request the entire $5.7 million the agency proposed to spend on lunar sample analysis. The Senate committee deletion would affect several hundred scientists at thirty universities, seven government-owned laboratories, and two independent laboratories. The Senate committee's action is especially noteworthy because it reflects a larger Congressional effort to decimate our country's space program. For example, the House of Representatives has voted to slash funding for a Jupiter orbiter-probe mission, for a solar-polar mission, and for the space telescope project. Just by itself, the Senate committee's vote provides a stunning indicator of how far the war against progress has gone. Having spent $30 billion to bring rocks back from the moon, we are not now willing to spend another $5.7 million to extract their scientific messages.

The number of new, technology-oriented business ventures in the U.S. is declining. For one thing, high tax rates have discouraged many entrepreneurs from taking the enormous gambles, and from putting in the enormous amounts of hard work, required to turn ideas into profitable businesses. Why struggle for years, only to fork over the bulk of one's reward to state and federal tax collectors? Moreover, thanks largely to government regulation the risks of entrepreneurship today are greater than ever. For instance, regulations change so often now that in some industries the chances are better than even that by the time a promising technology can be turned into a marketable product, that product will be banned from the marketplace for environmental or other reasons. Most importantly of all, high tax rates coupled with record-level government borrowings have siphoned out so much money from investors' pockets that in fact there is no longer enough money left in our economy to satisfy the financial requirements of those entrepreneurs who remain willing to try. According to a study published by the M.I.T. Development Foundation, 204 small, technology-oriented U.S. companies were able to raise money in 1969 by going public—by selling stock for the first time. In 1974, only four such companies were able to raise money by going public. And during the first half of 1975, according to this study, not a single such company was able to do that. Since then the situation has improved only marginally. Only forty-six small, technology-oriented companies were able to go public successfully in 1978. These numbers are especially worrisome in terms of employment. According to the U.S. Department of Commerce, new, technology-oriented companies create jobs much more rapidly than older, more established corporations. Indeed, a study conducted for the Commerce Department in 1976 showed that the average annual growth in the number of jobs was 40.7 percent for new, technology-oriented companies, compared with 0.6 percent for corporations described as "mature."

The decline in corporate profits is yet another indicator of how much trouble we are in. Given the outcry over the level of profits that U.S. corporations earned during the fourth quarter of 1978, it may come as something of a shock to learn that our corporations are actually becoming less profitable. But they are. In fact, the true picture is nothing at all like that 26 percent, fourth-quarter-to-fourth-quarter reported gain which grabbed headlines across the U.S. and which, in the words of the President's wage-price czar, "put business on trial in the eyes of the American people." If you adjust for the considerable impact of inflation on depreciation and inventory valuations—items that sound too technical to matter but that in fact are terribly important in calculating a company's financial status—you find that pre-tax corporate profits in 1978 were up only 10.7 percent from 1977. That's about the same as the rate of inflation itself; it shows that corporations, just like people, have been running harder just to stay in place. Moreover, as a percentage of gross domestic product in the U.S., corporate profits in 1978 were only 5 percent, which is actually lower than in 1977. Indeed, the average return to industry from 1947 through 1965—before the war against progress really began—was 8.6 percent.

These numbers suggest that for the U.S. economy to regain its health, corporate profits will have to rise sharply from their present level. After all, it is these profits that make possible the investments that in turn create new jobs. But the enemies of progress are determined to prevent any rise in corporate profits. The proposed "windfall" tax on oil-company profits is a forerunner —and a very scary one indeed—of the kind of thing we can expect as they escalate their anti-profit campaign. For one thing, it is utterly senseless to single out the oil industry for punishment. Why? Because—and this can easily be checked out; the numbers are public—the U.S. oil industry is among our country's least profitable industries. In terms of profits as a percentage of revenues, its "margin" in 1978 was only 4.5 percent, compared with 5.25 percent for all U.S. industry. (High-profit industries include soft drink companies, which had a 1978 profit margin of 7.8 percent, cosmetics makers, which enjoyed a 1978 profit margin of 8.1 percent, and drug manufacturers, which in 1978 reported a profit margin of 10.1 percent.)

Moreover, the "windfall" tax on oil companies is senseless because these companies do not deserve to be singled out for punishment. If anything they should be singled out for praise, and held up as a shining example of capitalism at its very best. In fact these companies have been working hard, and with considerable success, to help American consumers through the energy crunch with as little pain as possible. This is not a wild-eyed opinion; it is a dollars-and-cents fact. Despite all the recent price hikes, today a gallon of gasoline costs less than half as much in the U.S. as it costs in Western Europe or Japan—where oil is controlled by government-owned companies.

And finally, the "windfall" tax on oil companies is senseless because in no conceivable way will this tax bring more oil out of the ground. It is increasingly expensive to find oil, to drill wells, to build pipelines and refineries, and to transport oil to gas stations around the country. The more money that oil companies must pay out in taxes, the less they will have available to spend. And so the less fuel that will be available to consumers. The fact of the matter is that the "windfall" tax on oil companies has nothing whatsoever to do with solving the energy crisis. It is nothing but a very clever way to siphon out more money from our pockets without actually hitting us with yet another hike in our income taxes.

Make believe for a moment that you are the President. You

want to collect more money from those who earn it, so you can give more money to those who haven't got as much. But if you hike income taxes—again—the voters will scream for your political hide. So you slap a "windfall" tax on oil companies, which nobody likes anyway because you have brilliantly managed to blame these companies for the gas shortage. Of course, to pay this "windfall" tax the companies will raise the price of gasoline— if they've got to pay it, they've got to collect it. Consumers will fork over this extra money every time they tank up, and their hatred for the oil companies will increase. And the companies will immediately turn over this money to the government. Bingo! You've done it! You have gotten the money and the oil companies —your involuntary collection agents, as it were—have gotten the blame. With any luck at all, voters won't realize how badly they have been had. So now you can slap a "windfall" tax on cars, on washing machines, on movie tickets, and on just about everything. What a great way to siphon out money without losing votes.

No matter how you look at it, the present outcry over corporate profit levels is nothing but an exercise in deceit by the enemies of progress. After all, corporate profits are not some sort of pirate's booty. They do not go into the pockets of those executives who manage the corporations that earn them. Nearly half of all corporate profits—in all industries, including oil—are siphoned out by government in the form of income taxes. And corporations use the profits that remain after taxes for a variety of purposes that are absolutely vital to making progress: buying new machinery and equipment, building new facilities, and paying out dividends to those who do own our corporations—the shareholders, not the managers—as a reward for having made these profits possible in the first place by investing some of their money, rather than spending all of it at once on consumer goods and services.

And lastly, the most ominous sign of all that the covert war against progress has begun to take its toll. It is becoming harder now for Americans who are on the bottom rungs of the economic ladder to move up. For example, today the gap between black and white family income in the U.S. is beginning to widen. In 1965, the median income of black families came to about 54 percent that of white families. By 1976 this key figure had risen to 62 percent—by no means high enough, but obviously higher than it used to be. But since 1976 the trend has been going in the opposite direction. By the end of 1977 the median income of black families had dropped to 59 percent that of white families, and by the end of 1978 it was down to 57.1 percent.

There is hardly any mystery about why this gap has begun to widen. It is not a matter of cultural differences, of personal laziness, or even of welfare fraud. It is a matter of economics and of opportunity. When a country's rate of progress starts to decline—when corporate profits are held down, when entrepreneurs are unable to raise money, when research and development programs are slashed, when technological innovations are blocked—it becomes increasingly difficult to create enough new jobs. Upward mobility stops. Those who are caught on the middle and lower rungs of the economic ladder become stuck where they are. Some inevitably begin to slip down. And those who are on the bottom rung of the ladder get pushed off.

CHAPTER

5

Who and Why

CHAPTER FIVE

The war against progress is being fought by people who themselves enjoy a high standard of living, and who believe that to protect their own comfort they must prevent others from becoming equally comfortable. In other words, this is a war which has been mounted by a small group of "haves" against all the "have-nots." In this sense, the war against progress is different from the vast majority of wars that have ever been waged. For the supreme objective of the attacking army in this struggle is not to bring about any kind of change. Rather, it is to keep things just the way they are. To be sure, those who are fighting to undermine economic growth, technological innovation, and scientific research will never admit that in fact their objective is the preservation of the status quo. Indeed, they will deny it heatedly. But when you consider who these people are, and what precisely they are saying, the conclusion becomes inescapable that we are in the midst of a deliberate effort by individuals who have already climbed the tree of progress—or who are at the top by virtue of their parents' efforts— to keep its fruits for themselves by pulling up the ladder behind them.

No one has ever been drafted or Shanghaied into the army that is waging war on progress. It is a wholly volunteer outfit. Political leaders, high-level bureaucrats, university professors, writers, social activists such as movie stars and recording artists, habitual protestors who are always in the market for a noble cause—they have all joined willingly, even eagerly. Of course, theirs is not an army in the formal, military sense of the word. There are no ranks, no uniforms, no forts, no organized regiments, battalions, or platoons. And so, obviously, there are no personnel records from which to derive statistics concerning age, education, income, and so forth. But there are times when all that is required to form an accurate picture of a group is common sense and a willingness to see the obvious. And this is one of those times. For while the soldiers in this army do vary from one another in many ways, their similarities are much more striking than their differences.

Virtually all of these people have enjoyed the benefits of a good education. Many of them hold one or more graduate degrees from our most expensive and prestigious universities. But all too often their formal educations have been untempered by practical experience, with the result that they mistakenly equate life on the campus with real life. They fail utterly to recognize and to appreciate the differences. Nevertheless, because these people are well educated, they are either affluent or capable of becoming affluent at their convenience. And it is their failure to appreciate this capability—this ready access to money—that so totally discredits these people. Those among them who remain poor, do so by choice. For these privileged individuals, poverty is not a hideous, desperate condition that destroys the body and drains the spirit. Rather, it is a game that can always be stopped when it becomes tiresome, or when the lack of money starts to be a nuisance.

They consider work to be a form of entertainment, rather than a means of survival. They are utterly contemptuous of those who labor year after year, at jobs that are uninteresting and tedious, simply to earn enough money to feed and clothe themselves and their families. These people only take jobs they like. And the jobs they like best are never those in industry. They much prefer to work in the arts, at universities, for foundations, on the staffs of public-interest groups, or for local, state, and federal government agencies. They prefer not to notice that the money to support the arts, and to run these organizations and agencies, comes entirely from those individuals and institutions that are primary targets in the war against progress—taxpayers, investors, and the business community.

These people devote their considerable energies largely to the pursuit of pleasure. They have the freedom to do it. After all, these people are not bogged down by the mundane problems that are the fabric of daily life for working people, such as looking for a second job, shopping for a crib that doesn't cost the world, or figuring out how to pay the auto-insurance bill and also get the washing machine repaired in the same month without having to borrow money. Intellectual stimulation is especially important to these people, and they devote a fair amount of their time to getting it. They are forever seeking out the latest novel, the newest foreign film, the hottest record album. They crave action and excitement in their intellectual pursuits, and so they are easily impressed by whatever is new and trendy, regardless of how shallow or bizarre it might be. Indeed, the more weird something is, the more they seem to like it. Whatever is old and considered to be normal—or, worse still, traditional—is of little interest to them. This may well be because their own sense of history and culture does not extend beyond last week. The only ideas that interest them are the ones they think of themselves.

They insist that they are driven forward by a burning zeal to "make things better." Yet they are more afraid of being bored than of being wrong. So they involve themselves in one glorious cause after another; sometimes in several causes at once. Indeed, they seem to love causes more than people. And once committed to a cause, they work at a frenzied pace that leaves precious little time for careful analysis and reflection along the way. They are intelligent enough to quickly master the jargon of any issue, but they are too impatient to take the time required to truly understand what precisely is at stake. As a result they tend to be more glib than knowledgeable. They always wind up parroting the arguments and rhetoric of their leaders, and so they always sound more clever than convincing—except to one another. And as to the specific policies and programs which they advocate, they focus only on those consequences that affect them. They ignore those consequences that affect everybody else.

They claim to be "liberal." Yet they are appallingly, almost frighteningly intolerant of those who do not share their views. Indeed, there is no room whatever for doubters or dissenters in this army. And what precisely do these people believe? They believe that government is the people's best friend, and industry the people's worst enemy. They equate wealth with evil, poverty with goodness, and moderation with apathy. They consider action to be more important than improvement, zeal to be more virtuous than skill, and good intentions to be more valuable than good results.

Most importantly, these people believe that there is such a thing as a limit to the amount of progress that a country can withstand, and that the U.S. has reached this limit. Economic growth is now too messy and too disruptive to tolerate. Technological innovation is now too dangerous and too haphazard to permit. Scientific research is now too risky and too frightening to allow. They believe, in other words, that we can no longer afford to go on the way we have been going; that we have got to stop now before it is too late. If we persist in trying to move forward we will bring the whole thing crashing down on top of us. Progress? Of course we believe in it. Certainly we support it in principle. But it simply isn't possible right here, right now. Not any more. We have already gone as far as we can safely go. So we have got to slow things down. Indeed, we have got to stop moving forward and start to hold steady where we are.

Do not expect an enemy of progress to spell this out for you. He won't. He will always insist that his opposition to this particular project or to that particular policy is a thing apart, unconnected to whatever opposition there may be elsewhere to similar projects and policies. He will not volunteer to outline the philosophy that ties it all together. And this is why we have all been so slow to recognize the war against progress for the broad-based, long-range struggle that it really is. By focusing one at a time on the separate battles that comprise the overt war, and on the specific policies and programs that comprise the covert war, we have, so to speak, missed the forest for the trees. We have failed to see the thread—the philosophy—that ties together all the separate pieces. Yet this thread is there if only we are willing to look for it. To be sure, it isn't always easy to find. In fact, if you listen in on a conversation between someone who genuinely supports progress and someone who opposes progress, at first you may have some trouble figuring out which one is which. But if you keep in mind that progress comes from economic growth, technological innovation, and basic scientific research—and that each of these components is difficult, inconvenient, messy, and risky as hell under the best of circumstances—you will soon be able to identify the supporter of progress and the enemy of it. For instance:

"We've come a long way in this country, but we've still got a long way to go. We've got to give more people the opportunity to live the way they want."

"Absolutely. I couldn't agree with you more. I'm so very pleased to hear you talking this way."

"You realize, of course, that the only way to expand opportunities is to create new jobs."

"That's obvious."

"Then how about we go ahead and grant a permit to that corporation which wants to build a new factory on the outskirts of town. They seem like a responsible bunch."

"They certainly do, and it's a good idea. How soon will things get started?"

"Almost immediately, I should imagine. All they have to do for starters is to slice off about four acres from the forest and then—"

"Forget it. That forest is off-limits. My friends and I go backpacking there on weekends. And the river is fantastic for canoeing."

"Okay, so we won't let them build on that site. They said last week at a zoning board hearing that they could just as easily put up their factory on the land surrounding that old, boarded-up mansion the town's been trying for years to unload."

"No way. That place is a landmark. I don't want to tear it down to make room for a factory. I want to see it restored."

"You win. Forget the factory. Let the people in the next town give the corporation a permit to build there. But you know, we really ought to let some developer build new houses and apartments here. This way, when the factory does open and starts hiring, its employees will have places to live. Besides, if they come here to live it'll be good for our local businesses."

"You're kidding. This town is already too crowded, and you want to bring in more people? There's no way we could handle them without really lousing things up."

"You win again. Forget the new housing. But it's a good thing the university is planning to expand its laboratory and—"

"Not if I have anything to say about it. You want some blob escaping from the lab and heading for town?"

"Hey, come on. We're talking about a new lab for some of this country's most distinguished scientists. These guys don't go off half-cocked. Besides, in case you haven't noticed we've got a lot of construction workers around here who need jobs badly. Building that lab is important to them."

"I sympathize with these guys. I really do. But it's just too dangerous. In any case, a construction project like this one would mess up the neighborhood for a year. I'm against that totally."

"Speaking of messing up the neighborhood, I understand that one of the big oil companies is thinking about doing some exploratory drilling not far from here."

"How very typical of those profit-hungry criminals. Wouldn't you know that they'd show up here now that they've messed up every place else."

"I'm not crazy about it either. On the other hand, I'm even less crazy about the idea of running out of energy. You know, of course, that nuclear power is a lot cleaner. I'm beginning to wonder if despite Three Mile Island we should start to think about—"

"Forget it. You try putting up a nuclear power plant around here and you get demonstrations twenty-four hours a day. I'll lead them myself if I have to."

"Well, I suppose we'll just have to wait until totally new sources of energy become commercially available. I just hope we don't freeze to death in the meantime. In fact, I understand that there are several new companies working right now on promising

90

ideas. You know, high-technology companies."

"That's great. I really hope they succeed. We can use the money."

"What money?"

"The money they'll make if they succeed. We can tax it and then expand our income-transfer programs."

"Wait a minute. If you're going to tax this money, why should the people running these companies break their backs trying to earn it in the first place?"

"Look. Just because some people are willing to kill themselves working is no reason for them to get rich from it."

"But if nobody gets rich, where is the money going to come from to finance their ventures in the first place? How are they going to raise the money they need to get started?"

"You're talking details. I'm talking policy. It just isn't fair that some people have a lot of money while some people have very little money. I believe in equality."

"In other words, you'd be happier if all of us were equally poor."

"Look, I don't want to get into a big discussion about how the system works. I'm a social activist, not an economist."

"Come to think of it, what exactly do you do for a living?"

"Let's just say that I work to make things better."

"Better for you."

"Must you get nasty?"

"I beg your pardon. I meant no offense. It's just that you live in a lovely apartment, you dress well, you go skiing in Colorado every winter and you get to Europe at least once a year."

"That last trip to France was on business. I was doing research for my foundation."

"Don't be so touchy. I don't begrudge you an exciting business trip at all. I just mean to point out that the system you're so anxious to stop in fact treats you rather well."

"Material possessions don't mean that much to me. I can do without them."

"Easy for you to say when you already have them. The point is that even if you do give them up, you can always get them back again whenever you want. You have the education, the credentials, and the talent. Most people have to work like dogs for what they have. And they can't give up everything and then expect to get it back again. At least, not easily. These are the people who need the jobs you won't let be created."

"What I do, I do for them. It was my foundation that fought for higher unemployment benefits."

"If you and your colleagues hadn't also fought against the creation of so many new jobs, those people you're so anxious to help wouldn't have been unemployed in the first place."

"Boy, you do like to play with words. Maybe we can pick this up some other time. Right now, I'm running late."

"Sorry if I've held you up. Say, is this Porsche yours?"

"Sure. You like it? It's the supercharged model they came out with last year. It goes from zero to sixty so fast you wouldn't believe it."

"Terrific. Where exactly are you going?"

"Haven't you heard? They want to expand the airport. We're protesting on account of the noise."

"I've read some reports that the noise levels won't go up at all, or at least not enough so we would notice. But even if there is a bit more noise than before, I suppose that's part of the cost of progress. You do favor progress, don't you?"

"Absolutely. As I said before, I support it totally."

Well, so much for our "progressive" friend. Let him roar off to his noise-abatement rally. He has served his purpose, which is to illustrate that the war against progress is essentially a deliberate effort by a small faction of Americans who are themselves comfortable and affluent to pull up the ladder behind them. This is the objective. This is the common thread that connects all the overt and covert battles. And with a common thread to follow, it isn't hard at all to identify those interest groups and institutions that are part of the overall war. In short, they are those interest groups and institutions whose fundamental philosophy is to stop all forward movement; whose implicit or explicit objective is to turn the U.S. from its present role—as the world's most dynamic and powerful industrial civilization—into a quiet, clean, safe refuge for those privileged few who will be able to enjoy it.

The enemies of progress have fairly commandeered the environmental movement. To be sure, the environmental movement did not begin as the wholly negative, destructive force it is today. Not at all. It began as a prudent, intelligent, long overdue effort to insure that the physical disruption which inevitably accompanies progress would be kept to an absolute minimum. But this sensible and very welcome approach, along with most of those who espoused it, soon was swept aside in favor of an approach

93

that is far less moderate, far less open to compromise, far less practical—and totally incompatible with the requirements of making progress. Indeed, we must not for a moment forget that the environmental movement today is wholly different from what it started out to be.

Today the environmental movement is little more than a weapons system in the war against progress. Nearly all of the three hundred or so groups that comprise this movement are now working to prevent even the smallest amount of growth from taking place anywhere in this country. There is the Clamshell Alliance in the East, the Abalone Alliance in the West, and the First Society of Whale Watchers in Hawaii. New York has Ecology Action East, New Orleans has the Ecology Center of Louisiana, and San Francisco is home base for California Tomorrow. Other groups are the Sierra Club, Friends of the Earth, Friends of Nature, Friends of the Sea Lion, Friends of the Sea Otter, Concern Inc., Earth Awareness Foundation, Wilderness Watch, Citizens for Clean Air, and Citizens for Clean Water. In addition there are groups which call themselves Get Oil Out, Keep America Beautiful, the Environmental Defense Fund, and Ducks Unlimited.

One is struck rather forcefully by the names of these groups. Surely it is not a coincidence that in each and every case, the name conveys a purpose that no decent man or woman could possibly resent or oppose without suffering a pang of conscience. After all, who could have it in for the sea lion, the sea otter, nature, or the earth? Who does not want clean air and clean water? Who would not want to Keep America Beautiful? And who, for heaven's sake, would want to limit ducks? The specific goal of each group is invariably worthy and even noble when taken by itself—when disconnected from everything else and considered as a thing apart. The problem is that all of them combined inhibit progress and ultimately stop it completely. For example, the Council on Environmental Alternatives works "to encourage people to conserve, rather than consume, their environment." This sounds eminently sensible and prudent at first glance. But in practice it means don't drill for oil, don't dig for coal, don't build that factory, don't put up that housing development, don't start construction of that power plant—in short, we've gone about as far as we can safely go. So let's stop now before we bring the whole thing crashing down on top of us.

The enemies of progress have also seized control of our country's liberal political establishment. Traditionally, the liberal movement has been dedicated to the steady expansion of opportunity, of human dignity, and above all of freedom. It goals have been to raise standards of living everywhere and to secure, cherish, and defend the rights of man. The fact of the matter is that all of us owe a very great deal of what we have today—indeed, of what we are today—to this movement and especially to its earlier leaders. But in the last few years, the American liberal establishment has come to stand for very different things. Its present leaders are so obsessed with achieving equality of condition, that they would rather make a rich man poor than see a poor man become rich. They are so obsessed with avoiding risk, that to prevent it they are willing to eliminate all possibilities of reward for those who are not so frightened. And they are so obsessed

95

with preserving whatever they themselves already have, that they can think only of programs and policies that are designed to keep things just the way they are.

Today our country's liberal political establishment is devoted to siphoning out money from the economy, and to lowering the value of whatever money remains in the economy. This is neither an exaggeration nor a distortion of the record. If anything it is an understatement. It is the liberals who time and again raise taxes. It is the liberals who year after year vote for government budgets whose staggering deficits can be covered only by borrowing heavily in our cash-short capital markets. It is the liberals who have made the country so carefully, closely, and completely regulated that today our most distinguished scientists are blocked from conducting their research, our most daring and imaginative entrepreneurs blocked from lauching their ventures, our most productive corporations blocked from expanding, and we ourselves increasingly blocked from leading the kinds of lives we truly want. And finally, it is the liberals who have been keeping the monetary printing presses in high gear to provide the dollars to finance their policies and programs, which in turn has afflicted our country with one of the most virulent, debilitating bouts of inflation in our history.

The enemies of progress are more than selfish. They are also foolish. They fail utterly to understand what progress means and what it takes. And they are appallingly blind to what will happen should they ever manage to win their war. Indeed, they are so determined to protect their own comfort, so frightened by the dangerous world in which we live, and so unwilling to put up with any personal sacrifices that they have convinced themselves of three points, all of which are fundamentally wrong: First, that up to now progress has generally been an easy, pleasant, low-risk process. Second, that up to now progress has never really inconvenienced or adversely affected those who were already comfortable and affluent. And third, that a country can slam on the brakes at a given point in its history and then hold steady at that point for an indefinite period of time.

Progress has never been easy, and even more rarely has it been pleasant for those in the midst of it. And progress has never, ever been an undiluted blessing. The creation of new jobs and the expansion of opportunities have always been accompanied by a combination of by-products that are annoying, unpleasant, destructive, and sometimes absolutely frightening. There is simply no such thing as economic growth without construction and the accumulation of personal wealth, and therefore without some degree of mess and financial inequality. There is no such thing as technological innovation without danger, and therefore without some costly failures and terrible mistakes. And there is no such thing as scientific research without risk, and therefore without a goodly measure of concern about the outcome of experiments.

But progress and its various by-products are indivisible. We cannot separate the former from the latter, the way a thresher separates wheat from its husks. Either we take the by-products along with the progress, or we make no progress at all. It has always been this way, it is this way now, and it will always be this way. And because of this, throughout history a country's ability to make progress has depended largely upon the willingness of its people to tolerate the undesirable but unavoidable by-products of economic growth, technological innovation, and scientific research.

It is always the comfortable and affluent who suffer most directly from the undesirable by-products of progress. Create jobs in any city for people who had been unemployed, for instance, and you also create a demand for housing in that city's better, more attractive neighborhoods. After all, a man will not keep his family in a slum once he can afford to move them out. And when a city's good neighborhoods are deluged by an influx of families that are fleeing from its slums, the people who had been living all along in these good neighborhoods inevitably suffer a variety of inconveniences. Housing construction sites make these neighborhoods a mess. Shopping becomes less pleasant, because stores and their parking lots had been designed for fewer people. Indeed, traffic everywhere in these neighborhoods becomes heavier than it used to be. And all too soon local classrooms are over-crowded; to keep the quality of education from declining, new schools must be built and this of course will add to a neighborhood's disruption.

Clearly, then, the creation of new jobs is a mixed blessing. It triggers a welcome step upwards for the good neighborhoods' new residents—those who had been out of work and living in slums before the burst of economic growth that enabled them to escape. These people never had it so good. But for the good neighborhoods' older residents—those who had jobs all along, and who were comfortable and affluent prior to that burst of growth— the quality of life deteriorates in a variety of ways, as least temporarily. Life becomes less pleasant than it used to be. For these people, at least in the short run, "progress" is mostly a pain in the neck.

When working farms are sold to corporations as building sites, it is the comfortable and affluent who lose the most. These are the people who will no longer be able to take Sunday drives along empty roads that cut through miles of rolling field and pasture. Poor people do not own cars, after all, and most of them spend Sundays either looking for work or actually working at menial jobs because they need the overtime wages. And it is the comfortable and affluent whose weekend country homes will be less charming, and therefore less valuable, when these homes are surrounded by factories instead of apple orchards or dairy farms. Poor people don't own weekend country homes. And as more and more housing units are built for the people who will be moving out of inner-city slums to take jobs in these new factories, "the country" is pushed further and further away from the city. Going for a Sunday drive becomes a major project. And so, of course, does the effort required to travel to a weekend country home in an isolated rural area.

When wilderness regions are sliced in half by power lines, when architectural jewels are torn down to make room for buildings that are functional but esthetically revolting, when scientific breakthroughs force fundamental changes in our understanding of the universe and our ability to control life itself— once again, it is the comfortable and affluent who suffer the most. These are the people who can afford to visit the wilderness and to actually see the Furbish lousewort and the black-footed ferret while camping or canoeing down wild rivers on lazy summer weekends. Poor people spend their summer weekends sweating on the porches of their shacks, or seeking relief from the heat on the fire escapes of their city apartments. The survival of the Furbish lousewort and the black-footed ferret is of little concern to them. They are too pre-occupied with the mundane problems of life, such as paying the next month's rent. And neither can poor people afford the luxury of appreciating fine old buildings, and of fighting nobly to preserve them. A taste for architecture and a passion for its preservation are avocations for people with time and money to spare—and who already have jobs. Likewise with concern for the philosophical problems that accompany basic scientific research. Certainly these problems are serious, and worthy of careful attention. We must never ignore them. But we must also keep in mind that the only people who can afford to grapple with the philosophical aspects of research are those who are sufficiently comfortable and affluent to have the time for it.

Comfortable and affluent Americans have traditionally been willing to suffer the undesirable by-products of progress. This is not to say that they have always done so cheerfully and without reservation. Quite the reverse. We are dealing here with human beings, not with saints. Our comfortable and affluent have always moaned and groaned and screamed bloody murder whenever the time has actually come to run a risk, to accept the dangers of a new technology, to shove over and to make room for those fighting their way up the ladder of progress. But the record shows that throughout the history of our country, when confronted squarely with the choice of either stopping progress or putting up with it, our comfortable and affluent people have nearly always chosen to put up with it. Cheerfully and eagerly? Never. Grudgingly and with little grace? Usually.

But actions are what count. And the fact is that comfortable and affluent Americans have nearly always decided in favor of progress. In just about every instance, they have recognized and accepted an obligation to face new dangers and to shove over and make room for those less comfortable and affluent, just as others once faced dangers and shoved over to make room for them. It is this traditional—and when you stop to think about it, quite remarkable—willingness to tolerate the risks and inconveniences of progress that has enabled our country to come so far, so fast. To be sure, charity and a sense of fair play have had very little to do with it. Our comfortable and affluent people have traditionally supported progress because they have always understood that the alternative to progress is less attractive than the by-products of progress. More precisely, they have always understood that the preservation of their own standard of living rested utterly upon the ability of more and more people to achieve that standard for themselves. In other words, they have always understood that the alternative to moving forward is falling backward.

This attitude of enlightened self-interest has not disappeared. Today a majority of comfortable and affluent Americans continues to support progress. Indeed, it is business executives, investors, and high-income families who are most strongly resisting those relatively few comfortable and affluent Americans who are waging the present war. But a disorganized majority can easily be defeated by an organized and ferociously determined minority, and this is

101

the present danger. If the war against progress continues, those who are waging it will win. And if this selfish and short-sighted minority is in fact victorious, the result will be a chain reaction whose victims will include not only the poor, but the comfortable and even the very rich. No one—absolutely no one—will survive unscathed.

CHAPTER

6

If the War Continues

CHAPTER SIX

There is no need to guess what will happen if the war against progress continues. For this is not the first time that such a war has ever been fought. In fact a very similar one took place seven centuries ago in Western Europe. And by taking a brief glance backward to that earlier struggle, we can get a fairly good idea of how the present one is likely to conclude if it proceeds along its current course.

Contrary to what we learned in school, the Middle Ages was one of history's most inventive and progressive eras. A number of experts contend that in fact the first industrial revolution occurred during the Middle Ages, and this rather startling contention is supported by quite a bit of solid evidence. For example, between the tenth and thirteenth centuries there was a prolonged technological boom in Western Europe. Machines such as camshafts began to boost productivity among workers in the textile, paper-making, and food processing industries. The invention of the mechanical clock gave shape and structure to the day. And as scientists and engineers developed and deployed new sources of power, such as mechanized water mills, per capita consumption of energy began to rise dramatically across the European continent.

Industry grew rapidly during this age of innovation and unregulated capitalism. And as it did, the general standard of living rose. Scientific breakthroughs and technological innovations in agriculture, such as the "three-field" system and the heavy-wheeled plow, enabled farmers to more than double the amount of food they were able to produce. This increase in the food supply made possible a swift and steady growth of the population. Moreover, opposition to economic expansion was virtually non-existent. As a result new colonies were constantly being founded, while older towns and cities were steadily enlarged to make room for more and more people. According to Jean Gimpel, a French historian who has written extensively—and brilliantly—about the Middle Ages, "The period was characterized by a sense of optimism, a rationalist attitude, and a firm belief in progress."

It did not last. Toward the end of the thirteenth century, the rationalism and optimism of the Middle Ages began to crumble. The role of government began to expand, taxes began to rise, and entrepreneurs became subjected to a growing number of regulations. An environmental movement developed whose leaders argued that the process of industrialization had already gone too far; that rivers were becoming too polluted and the air too filthy to breathe safely. A general resistance to change developed, and as it did the rate of inflation began to soar. Productivity dropped, and energy consumption began to level off. The population growth rate began to decline, class differences hardened, and upward mobility

—perhaps the single most striking social feature of the Middle Ages—ceased. Urban unrest and incidents of urban violence became common. Bank failures and currency devaluations occurred at an increasing rate. In the midst of all this, traditional moral values gave way to a new attitude of permissiveness. In growing desperation, many people turned from established religions to new and often weird cults. Standards of living stopped rising and leveled off. Then they began to drop sharply. They kept dropping. The decades that followed were marked by economic turmoil, famine, the Black Death, the Hundred Years' War, and political upheaval throughout the continent.

It would be silly to suggest that the twentieth century will end for the United States in exactly the same way as the thirteenth century ended for Western Europe. After all, history does not repeat itself precisely. On the other hand, it would be even sillier to dismiss outright any comparison between these two eras. The similarities are too striking to ignore; they are more striking even than the differences. So the question is not whether the United States will destroy itself by turning against progress. It will. It must. The question is what precisely this decline will look like. What will collapse first? How will it happen? What will fall apart next, and what after that? Who will get hurt? How? Who if anyone will survive? And finally, what effect will the decline of the United States have on the rest of the world?

These questions are easier to answer than one might think at first. For civilizations are built like machines. That is, they comprise a finite number of parts, each of which is connected to another in a certain fashion, and all of which work together in a certain way to achieve a certain result. Now, to destroy a machine you need not take up a sledge-hammer and smash every single part of it. To render the entire mechanism inoperative you need break just one key part. Moreover, it need not be the largest and strongest part that you destroy; you can wreck a machine just as totally by destroying its smallest or most delicate component. In fact, when a large and complex machine breaks down it is usually due to the failure of just one small or delicate component. Telecast of the first 1976 Presidential campaign debate between Gerald Ford and Jimmy Carter was stopped for more than an hour following the blow-out of a ninety-cent transistor.

So the enemies of progress do not need one stupendous blast, or one overwhelming triumph, to achieve their final victory. They need only to destroy one crucial part of the complex machine that drives our country forward. This, in turn, will render the entire machine inoperative. And as the machine lies idle, the delicate connections that hold our civilization together will begin to snap, one after another after another. At some point during this chain reaction—just where it is impossible to predict with any certainty —political leaders, bureaucrats, and social activists will begin to argue that the broken machine can never be repaired. They will insist that it would be easier and more efficient simply to scrap the old machine, and to replace it with a different model. Their proposed new model will be a badly flawed one. But we will not realize this until it is too late. Desperate for a workable solution, and at this point willing to try anything, we will in fact vote for the proposed new model. And in doing so, we will make the worst mistake in our country's history. Put another way, then, the war against progress will destroy the United States by bringing us to the point at which we will destroy ourselves.

Since basic scientific research is the most delicate and vulnerable component of progress, it will likely be the war's first casualty. Scientists are not like guided missiles. They cannot be programmed to fly along certain trajectories at pre-set speeds to strike at carefully selected targets. Scientists are brilliant, complex, inquisitive, utterly devoted, and totally independent characters. To work effectively they must be completely free to pursue their own ideas and instincts—to let their extraordinary imaginations soar, to talk with whomever they please, to read whatever they please, to go wherever they please, and above all to conduct whatever experiments they believe are necessary to expand their understanding of the universe. Science itself can flourish only in an atmosphere of unrestricted freedom. It is worth recalling an earlier point: that all the great scientific breakthroughs of this century have been achieved by scientists who at the time were working in democratic countries.

The surest way to destroy science is to regulate it. Regulation inevitably takes the form of applications, of hearings, of red-tape jungles, and of inspections by the regulators that become a monumental waste of everybody's time. All of this slows down the scientific process to a crawl. Moreover, regulation always works to inhibit and sometimes to weed out the most creative and productive individuals; it does this by trapping them in rigid categories and by forcing them down paths they don't want to follow. In short, regulation inhibits the flexibility that is required to accommodate the very finest of minds. And, of course, regu-

109

lation costs a lot of money. The more money universities and corporations are forced to spend to meet the costs of regulation, the less money that will be available to finance scientific research.

Most importantly, scientific research is far too complicated a process for any group of regulators to direct, however determined and diligent they may be. Those who would actually do the regulating—bureaucrats in federal agencies, members of city councils, boards of concerned citizens—can not possibly know enough to make sensible decisions. Indeed, there is really no such thing as a sensible regulatory decision in science, because science rarely if ever follows a clear course that someone sitting in an office can direct or even predict. For instance, a physicist may fail to achieve some breakthrough to which he has devoted half his working life. But his failure may well provide a biologist with the key he needs to unlock some puzzle that has been confounding him for a decade. A chemist in Boston may make an unexpected discovery that is useless to his own research, but which proves crucially important to a geologist in California. Regulate science and this vital sort of intellectual cross-fertilization swiftly collapses.

As the regulation of science and of scientists in the U.S. continues to increase, the number of research projects under way will continue to decline. More projects will be banned outright. And many projects that are allowed by the government will be voluntarily abandoned or cut back because the regulatory costs of completing them will be prohibitively high. As our universities and corporations continue to slash their research budgets, our best scientists will emigrate from the U.S. to pursue their experiments at universities and corporations in other countries. Ironically, it

110

was the freedom to work without restriction or interference that brought so many of the world's greatest scientists to the U.S. in the first place. As our most talented scientists flee to other countries, and as research budgets at our universities and corporations continue to decline, the quality of science-related education in the U.S. will begin to deteriorate. Whatever jobs do remain will be filled by second-rate individuals—or by first-rate individuals with second-rate educations. Today's sharp decline in the number of scientific breakthroughs achieved in the U.S. will become even more drastic.

When the number of scientific breakthroughs achieved in the U.S. becomes negligible—that is, when the war against progress has at last destroyed our scientific community—our country's rate of technological innovation will drop by a staggering amount. This must happen, because technological innovations are invariably the by-products of scientific breakthroughs. Entrepreneurs will become an endangered species. But no government agency will rush to their rescue; the plight of entrepreneurs will bring no tears to the eyes of our liberal politicians, our bureaucrats, and our social activists. These characters will be too busy trying to save the Furbish lousewort and the black-footed ferret. Soon our entrepreneurs will become an extinct species, for not even the strongest among them will be able to survive without a steady diet of scientific breakthroughs. The disappearance of entrepreneurs will bring an abrupt end to the start of new ventures and new companies. And as a result of this the flow of new industrial processes and products, which even now has been reduced to a trickle, will dry up completely.

111

As our rate of technological innovation plunges down towards zero, economic growth will become nearly impossible to achieve. In fact, our economy will begin to shrink. Since entrepreneurs will no longer be starting new businesses, no new jobs will be created for people to build factories. And of course, no new jobs will be created for people to work in these nonexistent factories. As fewer and fewer of these new jobs are created, the number of existing jobs will start to decline in industries that provide goods and services to job-holders. For example, the housing industry will be decimated because people without jobs will be unable to afford new homes. The furniture industry and the travel industry will wither. The automobile industry will become crippled because so few people will be able to afford new cars. The entertainment industry will go into a tailspin as fewer and fewer people will be able to afford records and movie tickets. Indeed, from one end of this country to the other, and in every segment of the U.S. economy, jobs will start to disappear. The unemployment rate will climb to record levels.

As the unemployment rate climbs, opportunities will evaporate for people to improve their lives by raising their standards of living. For the first time in our country's history the American dream—that things can and will get better—will cease to be a realistic one. Instead, things will begin to worsen. In the early stages of this long and horrifying slide, no two groups in our country will be affected in precisely the same way. However, each group in some way will be adversely affected. Only later, after the evaporation of opportunity has inflicted its special damage on each group, will all of us begin to suffer in the same fashion.

In the end, we will all go down together. Money, education, intellectual brilliance, privilege, friends in high places—none of these advantages will make the slightest bit of difference. Those who held first-class accommodations on board the *Titanic* drowned just as quickly when the big ship sank as those who had been traveling in steerage.

The poor will lose all hope of escaping from their poverty. As the unemployment rate inches upward, those among the poor who have jobs will lose them. And those who were out of work all along will discover that their chances of ever finding jobs have been reduced to nothing. As the unemployed and the unemployable poor attempt to anesthetize themselves from the misery and hopelessness of their circumstances, the use of alcohol and of narcotics in our cities will begin to rise from its already high level. And as the search for money with which to buy alcohol and narcotics becomes increasingly desperate, the crime rate will begin to shoot up from its already high level; it will go into orbit. More stores and apartments than ever will be robbed, more people than ever will be held up in the streets, more cars than ever will be swiped from parking lots. Poor neighborhoods will become increasingly dangerous places as their streets and alleys become littered with a growing number of derelicts and drug addicts. And today's appallingly high rate of arson in poor neighborhoods will go up even further, as more and more men and women burn out their apartments to collect insurance money—which they will then use to finance their worsening liquor and drug habits.

As both the unemployment and crime rates move up, it will become even more difficult than it is today for poor families to

113

function effectively, or even to remain united. A growing number of fathers and mothers will drink themselves to death, or die of drug overdoses. Others will be convicted for their crimes, and sent to jail. All of this will drastically increase household tensions, and of course the primary victims of this increase will be the children. More and more of them will receive less attention than they require, less parental guidance, less discipline. At the very least, the fate of their parents and of their friends' parents will destroy whatever incentive these children might have had to stay in school until they would be able to graduate. They will see no future for themselves even with diplomas, and in a way they will be absolutely right.

Juvenile delinquency will become a much more serious problem than it is today. This, of course, will further aggravate living conditions in our country's largest cities. For instance, as more and more teen-aged children sit around all day with nothing to do—unwilling to attend classes, unable to find work—it is inevitable that the birth rate will increase markedly. This, in turn, will trigger a jump in the population growth rate of precisely those people who will be hit the hardest by the country's worsening economic problems. As a result of this, poor families will have more mouths to feed just when their opportunities for earning money will be evaporating. Apartments will become more and more crowded as the number of people living in them increases, not only because the birth rate will be rising so rapidly, but also because young adults without jobs will be unable to maintain apartments of their own; they will have no choice but to remain at home with their parents, their younger brothers and sisters, and perhaps a few unemployed aunts and uncles as well.

As the war against progress continues to rage, poor neighborhoods will continue to deteriorate. However, the rate of deterioration will accelerate. A rise in unemployment will leave fewer and fewer tenants able to pay their rent each month. Some of these people will be forcibly evicted by their landlords. But since there will be no crowd of wage-earners waiting to take over these emptied apartments, and since vacant apartments draw no rent, many landlords will let their unemployed tenants remain where they are by extending credit at horrendous, often illegal rates of interest. This of course will drive the poor even more deeply into debt. At the same time, landlords in poor neighborhoods will start to suffer from a shortage of cash that will be far more serious than their present shortage. Even now it is just about impossible for many of these landlords—including those who are honest and who manage their properties with the greatest of skill —to finance building improvements or even to pay for normal maintenance work.

Soon it will be impossible for any landlord in these neighborhoods to manage his buildings profitably. From one end of poor neighborhoods to the other, elevators that break down will stay broken. Shattered windows will remain shattered. Leaky pipes will keep leaking, and refrigerators that blow their motors will not be repaired. Fuel to heat these buildings during the winter months will be burned as sparingly as the law allows—in many cases even more sparingly than the law allows. Newspapers and local television news commentators will explode with outrage and demand that the responsible landlords be fined and even thrown

115

in jail. But the problem can not be made to disappear so easily, for a landlord who cannot collect his rents simply cannot afford to purchase fuel for his tenants, regardless of the landlord's good intentions and business skill. As more and more apartments go cold, illness among the poor will increase; among infants and young children the mortality rate will rise sharply.

One by one, the components of an urban bomb will drop into place. Loss of jobs, loss of hope, increased use of alcohol and narcotics, soaring rates of crime, disintegrating families, a rise in juvenile delinquency, a rise in the birth rate, apartments that are increasingly crowded, buildings that are rapidly deteriorating—all of these dreary and familiar elements will combine to create neighborhoods that are larger, more decrepit, and incomparably more dangerous than any slums that exist today in this country. And as the all-too-fragile threads that connect the poor to the mainstream of society begin at last to snap, these neighborhoods will be transformed into powderkegs of discontent and human misery. One spark—one silly, easily avoidable incident on some steamy August night—is all that it would take to set off a chain of explosions that would destroy our largest cities more completely, and more irrevocably, than any nuclear attack that might ever be launched against us by any foreign enemy.

In an all-out effort to prevent this spark from igniting, our various governments will begin to pump money into poor neighborhoods at unprecedented rates. For example, welfare payments will skyrocket as unemployment among the poor increases. The food-stamp program will expand by leaps and bounds as the politicians scramble to prevent mass starvation in the world's foremost agricultural nation. New and costly drug rehabilitation programs will be launched. Police and fire department budgets will move steadily upward in response to the soaring rates of crime and arson. There will be a sharp rise in the amount of public money made available to the poor for medical care. Urban renewal projects will become popular again, as part of a drive to relieve housing shortages caused by the rapid population growth among the poor. Indeed, all kinds of neighborhood-improvement schemes will be proposed and heavily funded by our various governments —not really in hopes of improving poor neighborhoods, but rather as a means of pumping money into these neighborhoods by creating non-productive, make-work office and "planning" jobs for hundreds of these neighborhoods' unemployed and unemployable residents.

As always, working Americans will foot the bill. Advocates of tax reduction will be swept aside as the need grows desperate for more and more government money to support the poor—or rather to contain the poor. Not out of compassion for these people, but out of cold fear for what would happen if their plight is ignored, working Americans will reluctantly agree to shell out to the tax collector even more of their earnings than they shell out today. And since the country's poor population will be growing at a faster rate than the non-poor population, each working American in effect will wind up supporting a growing number of dependents. Obviously, all of this means that as the war against progress continues, working Americans will be left with even less money in their pockets and in their savings accounts than they have today to spend on goods and services. More importantly, whatever money does remain in people's pockets will be worth less, as the government continues to cheapen the real value of each dollar by printing more and more of them to supplement the dollars it collects through taxation.

The long slide backward will begin. Already the excessive printing of money has triggered an inflationary spiral, which in turn has made it nearly impossible for working people to improve their standard of living. Those among us who work harder than we used to, do not put in this extra effort in hopes of reaping a bigger reward; we do so simply to keep from losing whatever we already have. But the devastating impact of today's inflation is merely a prelude to what will happen if the war against progress continues. Today the effects of inflation are mostly internal or invisible. That is, they either take place within the walls of our homes or they take the form of things we no longer do. We eat spaghetti more often than steak. We leave our basements unfinished because we cannot afford paneling and carpeting. We tune our pianos once every two years, instead of twice a year. And increasingly we are forced to spend our vacations at home, puttering around in our backyards, instead of driving to the mountains or the seashore, or flying off to Europe.

Within a very few years, the effects of inflation will become more visible—and sometimes permanent. Not only will our pianos remain untuned, but in our efforts to economize we will simply discontinue the children's lessons. We will buy as few new clothes as possible, and we will start to look a little ragged around the edges. We will abandon our habit of trading in the family car every third year and replacing it with a new one. Instead we will

118

make whatever repairs are absolutely necessary to keep the old wreck rolling. Our weekly night out at the movies will cease to be a tradition; we will save our money only for blockbuster films we are sure we will enjoy. We will eat out only when there is an event to celebrate, such as a birthday or an anniversary. And even then we will avoid fancy restaurants that charge extra for the blue-cheese salad dressing. We will cut back on magazine subscriptions, and increasingly we will wait for best-sellers to show up in our local libraries instead of rushing out to buy them in hardcover or even in paperback editions.

Middle-class neighborhoods will start to deteriorate almost as rapidly as poor neighborhoods. For even those of us with jobs will not have enough money to maintain our houses properly. We will have no choice but to postpone all repairs except those we must make immediately, for example when the pipes burst after freezing. Power lawnmowers that break will remain broken; manicured lawns are desirable but not necessary. When cracks appear in the driveway asphalt, we will fill them in with dirt rather than repave. Likewise with our roofs; when they leak we will patch them up as cheaply as we can, rather than replace them as we should. And when the spray attachment to the kitchen sink faucet breaks again—to hell with it, we can live without spray attachments. Within a remarkably short period of time, five to six years at the outside, houses in our country's middle-class neighborhoods will start to show the effects of cheap repairs and postponed maintenance. The neighborhoods themselves will quickly go to seed.

The structure of our family lives will change dramatically. As the need for cash grows critical, more and more men who are heads of households will be forced to take second jobs. Wives who are already working will themselves take second jobs, and wives who are not now working will go to work. To make all this job-holding possible, a network of day-care centers will develop that is far more extensive than the network which exists today. And we will not park our children at these centers merely for a few hours each day, but rather for the entire day and for much of the evening as well. We may even be forced to adopt the practice of parents in some East European countries, who leave their children at "day-care" centers from Monday morning to Friday afternoon and who retrieve them only for the weekends. In time a large percentage of our children will be raised by "professionals" rather than by parents. For a few children, this may be something of an improvement. But for most children it will be an unhappy, unsettling experience with many more draw-backs than benefits.

Our older children will also start to suffer. As the shortage of new jobs becomes critical, fewer and fewer young adults will be able to leave home and live independently. Those who are academically inclined will remain in school for as long as possible —a tactic that will postpone the collision with reality but that will also increase the financial pressures on the parents of these students. Young adults who are not academically inclined will simply remain at home, idle and unemployed; their understandable un-happiness will contribute mightily to a rise in family tensions. All children of working Americans, whatever their academic accomplishments may be, will be forced to live with one set of parents or the other after marriage. In the first place, many young couples will not be able to afford apartments or houses of their own. And of course those spreading bans on housing construction will make it increasingly difficult even for young couples who can afford places of their own to find them.

Over time, then, a growing number of American homes will be occupied by two generations of the same family. And if the younger generation succumbs to that most powerful tendency of poor and frustrated couples the world over—to have children they cannot afford to support—many American homes will be occupied by three generations at once. Sociologists no doubt will applaud this development, and many will make great names for themselves writing and lecturing about the benefits of the multi-generational living experience. But for those involved—older Americans who will be denied their privacy; younger Americans who will be denied their independence—the daily business of living will be marked by growing tensions and extreme unhappiness.

Conditions will steadily worsen. As the country's economic growth rate continues to drop, more and more working Americans will inevitably lose their jobs. Architects, electricians, bricklayers, and carpenters will find themselves on unemployment lines, for instance, because entrepreneurs will no longer be building factories and because real estate developers will no longer be building apartments and houses for the would-be employees of these nonexistent factories. Auto workers will be laid off by the thousands because so few Americans will be buying new cars. And hard times in the auto industry always lead to unemployment in the steel industry, which in turn puts pressure on the coal-mining industry. Roofers and plumbers will go out of business because more and more of their customers will either stop maintaining their properties or start maintaining these properties themselves. Piano tuners and piano teachers will go broke, and so too will the owners of summer camps and vacation resorts. For the first time in our country's history, working people will cease to be upwardly mobile. Instead, we will become either frozen in place or downwardly mobile.

As for the very rich in this country, they will become increasingly idle as the war against progress continues to rage. They will have no incentive whatever to invest their money in job-creating ventures, such as new corporations, because the taxes on whatever profits they might earn will be too high to justify the risk. Indeed, even at today's tax rates an individual who invests $1,000,000 of his own money into a new venture which is managed so competently that after only two years it turns a $100,000 profit, can wind up with an after-tax profit of less than $20,000. Should this same $1,000,000 be used to buy government securities, it would earn tax-free interest totaling more than $120,000. In fact, as the war against progress destroys scientific research and technological innovation, it will be literally impossible for rich people who genuinely want to invest their money in job-creating ventures to do it. For there will be no such ventures in which to invest. Increasingly, rich Americans will plow their money into nonproductive, highly speculative commodities such as jewelry, works of art, and even rare wines.

For the first time in our history, the United States will be afflicted with an upper class that is either unwilling or unable to be productive. The most vital contribution of any upper class to its country's welfare—money—will cease to be available for projects that would enable economic growth. Moreover, the entrepreneurial skills of our wealthy individuals, which in many cases is precisely what made them wealthy in the first place, will lie unused. In short, the war against progress will force the creation of an upper class in this country that is idle and indulgent, rather than busy and productive. Before long it will come to resemble the upper classes of France during the reign of Louis XIV and of Russia under Nicholas II—useless, sybaritical, totally isolated from the daily life of the country to which it belongs.

Within a decade's time, should the war against progress continue at its present clip, the three economic classes that together form the American civilization will have pulled irrevocably apart from one another. The poor will have abandoned all hope of ever joining the working class; they will be little more than prisoners in urban ghettos that will be maintained with money collected through taxation from people who work. The working class will have been crushed by the financial burden of maintaining the poor, or rather of containing the poor; and their resentment of the poor will rise toward the boiling point as their own cherished standard of living drops. And the rich will have been forced to turn themselves, their capital, and their considerable talents to the pursuit of non-productive pleasures. We will become a nation of three separate and disconnected classes, each locked on a self-destructive course and each living in dangerous and sullen isolation from the other two.

As the fabric of American civilization unravels, the complex problems that even today confront and confound our country will worsen. For example, in the absence of scientific break-throughs and technological innovations, we will be unable to provide enough energy to keep our industries operating, to keep our homes warm, and to keep our cars tanked up. Current efforts to conserve energy merely by using less of it, such as the law which limits our driving speed to fifty-five miles per hour, are intellec-tually satisfying but useless in a practical sense. We can never solve the energy crunch solely by using our present equipment slightly more carefully; we can do it only by discovering new supplies of energy and by developing new equipment that is structurally more efficient than whatever we are using today. For instance, we will need to develop new auto-body materials that are every bit as strong as steel but that weigh less, and auto engines whose fuel consumption rates are regulated by built-in microprocessing units. At the same time, we will need to develop new techniques for recovering every last drop of oil and every last cubic foot of natural gas from our present wells, and every last ton of coal from every working mine. And of course we will need to develop wholly new sources of energy, such as solar power and laser fusion power. But none of these developments will be possible once scientific research is destroyed, once technological innovation becomes impossible, once the country's economic growth rate plunges down toward zero. And as the supply of available energy dwindles due to the lack of new scientific break-throughs and new technologies, even more jobs will evaporate as businesses curtail their operations or shut them down completely for lack of fuel.

Our environment will deteriorate horribly as the components of progress wither under sustained attack. Without scientific research, we will not be able to develop energy sources that are cleaner than oil and coal, safer even than nuclear power. Without technological innovations, we will not be able to produce equipment that is capable of cleaning up environmental disasters such as oil spills and noxious smoke from industrial facilities. And without robust economic growth, corporations will not be able to earn the money they will need to purchase and install the incredibly expensive machinery that can reduce or eliminate pollution. In 1978, the National Commission on Water Quality estimated that public and private capital expenditures needed to meet present water pollution control laws could total as much as $670 billion. Obviously, corporations will have to earn this money before they can spend it. And even now the war against progress is eating away at their earnings. As the war continues, then, our rivers will grow more polluted and our air increasingly unsafe and unpleasant to breathe.

Most ominously of all, the war against progress will cripple our present drive to end racial discrimination in the United States. For economic growth has always been the single most powerful and effective enemy of racism. The more opportunities we have to live the way we want, the less bothered we are by other people. More precisely, the wealthier we become the more tolerant we become of others. After all, one is much more likely to be friendly when things are going well than when things are terrible. In the decades after World War II, more than any other factor it was the economic development of the South that enabled black

Americans to begin their long journey down the road toward genuine equality. In fact, throughout the history of this and every other country racial discrimination has lessened during periods of robust economic growth. So it is inevitable that as the war against progress continues, and makes growth impossible to achieve, racial tensions in the U.S. will rise. It is even possible that many of the gains earned by minority-group Americans during the booming 1960's will be wiped out entirely.

Our national character will undergo a radical change. There is no way to prove this with statistics, but it's a fact that throughout our history, we Americans have been an exceptionally open and friendly bunch of people. The surliness, the sourness, the crankiness that is the mark of people in so many other countries has always been notably absent in the United States. For two centuries foreign visitors to our shores have been struck by this phenomenon; it is among the first things that an alert American notices when traveling abroad, especially for the first time. This traditional openness and friendliness of ours is hardly the result of some lucky genetic fluke. It is the direct result of our progress. In a country where opportunities are steadily expanding, people operate on a set of perceptions whose natural products are openness and friendliness: First, that each person is getting a fair shake. Second, that each person can in fact move up. And third, that each person's progress is the product of that person's effort or initiative; it has not come at the expense of anybody else.

This set of generous perceptions will not survive. When the war against progress has destroyed equality of opportunity—when it has totally undermined the connection between work and reward—we Americans will grow more sullen, more sour, more downright nasty toward one another than we have ever been before. As opportunities contract, as standards of living drop, as the notion evaporates that things can and will get better as the reward for personal effort and initiative, each of us will start to feel exploited. Now this is not to say that each of us will be absolutely or even moderately correct. But when people grow angry and frustrated, emotions tend to override cool reason and analysis. When the crunch hits home, each of us will become so obsessed by our own problems that we will be utterly blind to everybody else's problems. All too easily we will each convince ourselves that we are the ones who are bearing the brunt of the war's effects. And each of us will start to look out for himself and herself with a ferocious vengeance. We will have no choice but to do this. When opportunities start to contract—when the same number of people start scrambling for slices of a shrinking pie, so to speak—each person looks upon everybody else as a dangerous competitor. Each one fights like the dickens to keep his own slice to himself.

Our growing antagonism toward one another will show up most visibly at work. For it is at work that people who feel exploited can most easily vent their anger and frustration without directly hurting members of their own families. Blue-collar workers in our major industrial factories, and hourly-wage employees throughout our economy, will become more insistent than ever about "working by the rules." Increasingly they will refuse to start one minute earlier than necessary, or to work at a pace that is the slightest bit faster than the rules require. And when the time comes to quit for the day, they will drop their tools, or they will walk away from customers in the middle of conversations, and be out the door on their way home even before the whistle stops blowing or the clock stops chiming. White-collar workers will become every bit as churlish. They will begin to treat their own subordinates like dirt. And in a horribly misguided effort to protect their own standards of living, they will form unions that will be even more militant than those to which blue-collar workers belong. Increasingly we will see professional people such as managers, engineers, and teachers refusing to show up early or stay late. In short, all of us will cease taking those extra steps, and cease going those extra miles, that together have helped to drive our country forward so far and so fast.

It is this selfish attitude—this narrow-minded, looking-out-for-Number-One approach to life—that will send our country into its final tailspin. Rank-and-file union members, desperate to stabilize their declining standard of living, will demand that their elected leaders push management harder than it has ever been pushed before for higher wages and new benefits. This demand will put the leaders of our country's major unions, who in fact are among the most progressive and politically sensible union leaders in the world, under intense pressure to negotiate agreements they know full well will send the corporations with which they are negotiating into bankruptcy. But at this late date, union leaders who urge moderation will be summarily voted out of office. They will be succeeded by individuals who will be every bit as radical and short-sighted as the union members who elected them. These new leaders will then proceed to secure the contracts their constituents demand. Many corporations will balk, and a wave of lengthy and perhaps violent strikes will roll across the country. The press will side with the unions, as it usually does, and under intense public pressure a large number of corporations will cave in. And then they will go bankrupt.

Economic conditions will continue to deteriorate. For example, as the unemployment rate rises even more Americans will need welfare payments, unemployment insurance, food stamps, and Medicaid benefits. And our government's response to the deteriorating situation will only serve to make things worse: it will raise taxes once again, and it will start to print money at an even faster rate. As the inflationary spiral swirls with increasing speed, the fabric of our civilization will unravel at an accelerating rate. Indeed, it will start to shred. Tensions will reach the boiling point among our different economic, geographic, and racial groups. Working Americans will grow to hate the poor. Northerners will convince themselves that the flight of industry to the Sunbelt is the root cause of their problems. Black Americans will see their hard-won gains evaporate, and Hispanic Americans will be deprived of any chance at all to get ahead. Both goups will hold white Americans to blame for their troubles.

We will become our own worst enemies. Too angry and frightened to think clearly, we will convince ourselves that the situation is too critical to be ameliorated by half-measures, or by careful and deliberate modifications of our policies. We will demand nothing less than radical surgery—and we will get it. We will vote into power an Administration that is pledged to end the war against progress by whatever means may be necessary.

This Administration will not be content merely to defeat the enemies of progress. It will attempt to destroy them, and in doing so it will destroy the country as well. Its leaders will prohibit freedom of speech, in an effort to silence once and for all those who would speak out against science, against technological innovation, against growth. They will ban the freedom to assemble, in an effort to stop those mass rallies that the enemies of progress use so effectively to fight their battles. And they will subject our newspapers and television news departments to government censorship of the strictest sort, to deprive the enemies of progress of all publicity and sympathy for their aims.

The leaders of this Administration will describe themselves as saviors of the capitalist, free enterprise system. And without exception, they will look like business executives, sound like business executives, and in every way give the impression that their instincts and sympathies lie wholly with restoring the free market to its central role in our economy. But in fact the leaders of this Administration will subscribe to the notion that our country's problems are so huge and intractable that corporations and investors working together—in other words, the free market— would simply be unable to solve them. So in the name of restoring the free market, the leaders of this Administration will develop policies and programs that will irrevocably destroy the free market by positioning Big Government at the center of our economic system.

In a last-ditch effort to revive our economy as rapidly as possible, this Administration will seize control of our largest and most productive corporations. Then it will launch a new government agency with the authority to control all research and development in the U.S., and also with the authority to manufacture whatever new products may emerge from this co-ordinated effort. Union contracts that this Administration believes are inflationary will be set aside, and corporation executives who refuse to lower the prices of their companies' products to levels the government declares to be correct will be thrown into jail without trial; our Congress will eagerly vote the enabling legislation for these actions. At the same time, our countryside will be ripped to pieces in a crash program to find more energy and to build new power facilities to fuel what this Administration will refer to as the coming economic revival. Naturally these programs will be terribly expensive, and to finance them this Administration will impose new taxes and, of course, print more money.

Any resistance will be swiftly, mercilessly crushed. We will be told that these unprecedented intrusions into the free enterprise system are absolutely necessary; that the economy is too weak to be left in the hands of business executives. Moreover, we will be assured that all these violations of our basic freedoms are only temporary, and that the dictatorship we have ourselves installed will be dismantled voluntarily once the situation has improved. But of course the situation will not improve. It will continue to deteriorate. And in any case there is no such thing as a temporary dictatorship. We will be unable to regain our lost freedoms, and without them we will be unable to make any progress at all. In short, then, by allowing the war against progress to continue until the point when we are willing to elect an Administration that is pledged to end the war by whatever means may be necessary, we

131

will unwittingly bring about precisely that result which the enemies of progress are fighting to achieve: the destruction of the United States as the world's most powerful and progressive civilization.

7

Dragging the West
Down With Us

CHAPTER SEVEN

The destruction of the United States as the world's most powerful and progressive civilization will not be an isolated tragedy, like the sinking of a great ship somewhere in the middle of an ocean. For the U.S. is not an isolated country, unconnected to other countries and responsible only for her own welfare and security. Today we are part of a long and complex chain of countries that literally circles the globe. Many links in this chain are so small and weak that their destruction would be of little consequence to the whole chain; other links could easily be bent or stretched across whatever gap would be created. But as the most powerful and progressive civilization on earth, the U.S. is by far the largest and strongest link in this global chain. Our destruction would create a gap that would be too wide to close. The chain would be broken beyond repair, and many of its links would be crushed or permanently twisted as they snap back and fall in a heap.

Take just a brief look at the global role we now play, and you will quickly realize how utterly impossible it would be for any other country in the Free World to replace us; how quickly all of our allies would sink should we ourselves go under:

The United States is far and away the world's most dynamic, productive, and creative culture. More Nobel prizes for literature have been awarded to American writers than to writers of any other country. More of the world's innovative ballet companies make their home in the U.S. than in any other country. Symphony orchestras based in New York, Philadelphia, Cleveland, Chicago, Boston, and Los Angeles are universally recognized as among the finest anywhere. We have three of the world's best opera companies. More innovations in the field of popular music—ragtime, jazz, swing, rock and roll—have originated in the U.S. than in any other country. Even our fashion industry is a world leader, with a steady stream of triumphs ranging from Levis blue jeans to evening gowns by Calvin Klein. Indeed, in just about every cultural discipline it is Americans who are blazing new ground and setting the pace for everybody else.

The United States is the lynchpin of the world's communications system. For example, today more than a hundred countries have joined the world-wide network operated by the International Tele-communications Satellite Consortium, an organization whose very existence was made possible by the U.S. space program. This consortium has already opened communications links to parts of Asia, Africa, and South America; links that could not possibly have been opened any other way. Countries that stretch across large geographic areas, such as Canada and Indonesia, have vastly improved their own domestic communications networks by hooking up to satellites built by U.S. corporations and launched by the U.S. government. Business and international trade as we know it would be utterly impossible without these split-second, global networks. Even impoverished people in developing countries are now dependent on communications systems developed and maintained by the U.S. To cite just one example, the U.S.-built, ATS-6 experimental satellite is the key to a project now under way in India which provides medical and educational services to residents of that country's poorest and most remote villages.

The United States is the world's most important economy. This is because we are far and away the world's largest and most productive economy. Our gross national product, for instance, is twice as large as the G.N.P. of any other country. In fact, the budgets of some U.S. corporations are actually larger than the national budgets of most countries. It is obvious that the size and power of the U.S. economy has provided Americans with the highest standard of living on earth. What is less obvious is that people in other countries are also dependent on the size and power of the U.S. economy for their own rising standard of living; in some cases for their very survival.

For instance, each year dozens of foreign companies come to the U.S. to borrow the billions of dollars they need to finance new, job-creating projects. Why do they come here for money? Because they are unable to raise this money in their own countries, whose economies are just too small. Each year dozens of foreign governments come to the U.S. to borrow money to purchase food and fuel. Indeed, by loaning money to these governments—literally billions of dollars each and every year—U.S. banks today are helping to keep millions of people in developing countries from starving to death. After World War II, it was the U.S. economy which generated the money to rebuild Western Europe. And today, by serving as the world's largest market for both raw materials and manufactured products, it is the U.S. economy more than any other economy that is making it possible for countries such as Brazil, Nigeria, and Mexico to develop to the point where they can stand up by themselves.

Most importantly, the United States is the only country strong enough to block the Soviet Union's drive for global supremacy. Now this is not a question of simple-minded anti-communism, or of good-guys versus bad-guys. Rather, it is a question of how the world works. At any given point in history, one particular country—one particular civilization—reigns supreme. You may not like the idea, but you cannot deny it. The world has always worked this way, it works this way now, and it always will work this way. The Greeks, the Romans, Spain, France, England—these are among the countries and civilizations that have already had their turns. Earlier in this century Adolf Hitler tried to install his Third Reich in the lead position. For several decades now, it is the U.S. which has reigned supreme. In the very broadest terms, it is we who set the pace, make the rules, call the shots. So to speak, we are the incumbent.

Today the Soviet Union is challenging the incumbent. In other words, the Russians are struggling to replace the Americans as global leaders. To be sure, there is no way to prove this. In no Kremlin office is there a safe in which is locked the blueprint for a Soviet takeover from the U.S. But the record of Soviet behavior

138

suggests that this is what the Russians are attempting to do. Indeed, the record of Soviet behavior does not suggest anything else. In the late 1940's and 1950's, for example, the Russians conquered nearly all of Eastern Europe. They literally wiped off the map three independent countries in this region—Estonia, Latvia, and Lithuania—by absorbing them into the Soviet Union itself. Since the 1960's, the Russians have been fighting continuously for influence and territory in the Mideast, in Africa, and in Southeast Asia. Their string of victories in just the last few years has been nothing short of spectacular. Fighting either with their own troops or through proxy forces such as those of Cuba and East Germany, the Russians have installed friendly governments in no less than seven countries: South Vietnam, Cambodia, Laos, South Yemen, Afghanistan, Angola, and Ethiopia. More Soviet victories of this sort seem likely in the near future, for instance in South Africa and Rhodesia, where the Russians and their proxies are working actively to undermine the present governments.

Military power is the key to success for any country that seeks to become supreme by forcibly unseating the incumbent power. And this is why for many years now the Soviet Union has been embarked upon the most extensive, most expensive arms build-up in recorded history. As a result of this arms build-up—which is still going on—the Soviet Union has more than five times as many tanks as the U.S., four times as many artillery pieces, and three times as many submarines. It has more nuclear-tipped, inter-continental ballistic missiles than the U.S. And the Soviet air force has successfully tested rockets that are capable of catching U.S. observation satellites and of blowing them out of orbit—

an act of warfare specifically prohibited by treaty and one that would render the U.S. dangerously "blind" to the movements of Soviet missiles and troops.

The Soviet arms build-up has coincided with détente. It has taken place during precisely those years of the first strategic arms limitation agreement, called SALT-I. For about a decade now, U.S. defense expenditures have actually been declining at a rate of roughly 2 percent a year in constant dollars (that is, corrected for inflation). Soviet military expenditures during these same years have been rising at a rate of more than 6 percent a year. Today, although the Soviet economy is roughly half the size of the U.S. economy, the Russians are outspending us militarily by more than 20 percent a year. In other words, today they are spending for weapons and troops a percentage of their gross national product that is more than twice as large as the percentage we spend for weapons and troops. This is largely why the Soviet economy remains so weak. Today even Western analysts who are sympathetic to the Soviet Union concede that the Russians' accumulation of military hardware far exceeds any legitimate defense requirement.

So the Cold War really is a war. It was launched by the Soviet Union in the aftermath of World War II. Its objective is to topple the U.S. as the world's leader and to install the Soviet Union in its place. This is what the Russians are up to. This is the objective of their policies. And all of this suggests two facts that some Americans have been reluctant to face. First, the Russians will not be satisfied with any kind of "deal" that leaves the U.S. in control and the Soviet Union as a sort of junior partner. The

Russians are determined to unseat the U.S., and they are playing to win. Second, the Cold War can end in only one of two ways. Either the Russians will fail, or they will succeed. If the Russians do fail, then the U.S. will continue as the world's leading power. If the Russians succeed, they will proceed to impose their own system on all of us. And this must not be allowed to happen, because the system that the Russians impose on those whom they control—the system that as a dictatorship they must impose to keep control—is repugnant. It is inhuman.

Clearly, the most dangerous days of the Cold War are yet to come. The Soviet Union is not embarked on history's most extensive arms build-up for nothing. It is inevitable that in the coming years the Soviet Union will begin to unleash its awesome firepower against scores of weak countries in the Mideast, Africa, and Southeast Asia. Before long it is likely that the Russians will be taking aim at the very largest countries in these regions, and then at countries that belong to the industrialized world. And not a single one of these countries will be strong enough to defend itself against the Russians. Their only chance for survival will rest upon the strength and will of the United States to oppose the Russians with a combination of military, economic, and political strategies that together will be capable of blocking the Soviet drive for supremacy.

There is not the slightest possibility that any of our country's allies could fill the various gaps—military, economic, communications, cultural—that would be created by the destruction of the U.S. All of our allies put together have less military firepower than we have. All of their economies put together are weaker than our own. All of them combined lack the satellite-communications technology that we have. All of them combined do not equal a culture as dynamic, productive, and creative as our own. In any case, our allies are so distrustful and suspicious of one another that any possibility of a serious, co-ordinated effort to close the gap by combining resources is out of the question. Let us not forget that within this century two world wars have erupted precisely because our present allies have been unable to get along peacefully with one another.

In short, the Free World could not survive without the U.S. to lead it. There is no use bemoaning this, or wishing fervently that our country did not in fact occupy a central, irreplaceable role in the global scheme of things. And it makes little sense to argue—as the enemies of progress argue—that our country has no right to be so powerful and so important. It is not a question of rights. It is a question of history. One country always reigns supreme, and today it is the United States. This is not the product of luck. We have made ourselves what we are today, and we need not apologize for it. Of course we could be doing a better job of it. We are by no means perfect. But as a country—as a civilization— the good we are doing outweighs whatever harm we may be causing.

Today we are the Free World's leader not because we want this responsibility, but because no one except us can meet this responsibility. We and we alone have the power. We have the broadest shoulders. This is not a conclusion based on arrogance, or on flag-waving chauvinism, or even on genuine patriotism. It is a fact based squarely on the realities of the complex, dangerous

142

world in which we live. And it means that if the U.S. does not continue to lead the Free World—does not continue to preserve and even to enhance its strength—then the Free World itself will not for long survive.

The first to be dragged down by our own decline will be those people who live in the impoverished Third World. Droughts and other natural disasters, coupled with high birth rates, have already brought these people to the edge of catastrophe. According to the Commission on World Hunger, between 1980 and 1990 a staggering number of Third World citizens—1.2 billion people in thirty-six countries, or about 30 percent of the world's population—are likely to die of starvation. Since the only country capable of producing enough food to feed these people is the United States, our decline must inevitably seal their doom. Indeed, our decline will even seal the doom of Third World countries that are now capable of buying whatever food they need by exporting raw materials such as coffee, cocoa, bauxite, and copper. We are their largest market—their biggest customer—and when we can no longer afford to buy these raw materials they will no longer be able to earn the money with which to buy our food.

As the fragile economies of the Third World begin to shatter, the number of violent political upheavals in these countries is certain to increase. As it does the Soviet Union will intervene—either with its own troops or with Cuban and East German troops —to insure that the local politicians and generals who emerge victorious from these upheavals will be politicians and generals who are sympathetic to Moscow. In countries that produce raw materials, the restoration of order will be followed by massive

amounts of Soviet technological assistance to boost production of
these raw materials to record levels. At the same time, trade agreements will be signed to ship these products to the Soviet Union in
return for rubles or perhaps Soviet-made manufactured goods.
On the surface, then, Third World countries that succumb to
Soviet power will appear to benefit economically.

But Third World countries that trade with the Russians,
instead of with the U.S. and its allies, will be unable to prevent
mass starvation. Indeed, trading with the Russians will guarantee
mass starvation. Since rubles are utterly worthless in Free World
countries—which, let us remember, are the only countries that
produce enough food both to feed themselves and to export—
Third World countries that trade their raw materials for rubles
will be unable to buy food from those countries which have it to
sell. And Third World countries that receive Soviet-made manufactured goods in return for their raw materials will also be trapped;
these goods are grossly inferior to Western-made goods, and no
capitalist country will buy them for hard currency or trade its
food for them. As the population of the Third World is decimated
by starvation, those who remain alive will discover that they are
working primarily to supply the Soviet Union with the raw
materials it will need to fuel its own sluggish economy and to
support is own military forces.

It will not be long before the decline of the U.S. triggers the
economic destruction of today's rapidly developing countries.
For example, Brazil's efforts to achieve a high rate of economic
growth have been hugely successful up to now. But today the
success of Brazil's ambitious growth program rests largely on that

country's ability to develop world-scale, technologically advanced aircraft and micro-computer industries. However, the development of these industries in turn rests largely on the continued willingness of U.S. aircraft and computer companies to sell or otherwise to transfer their own technologies to their fledgling Brazilian counterparts. Of course, the rate at which a company transfers its technologies rests largely on the rate at which it can develop new technologies to replace the ones it sells; after all, you cannot expect a company to transfer its latest designs to a potential competitor. So as the rate of innovation in the U.S. continues to decline, so too will the rate at which Brazilian companies will be able to acquire the technologies they must have to grow. And when the growth rates of Brazil's aircraft and micro-computer companies begin to decline, that country's carefully timed, delicately balanced development plans will crumble. Other rapidly-developing countries will be caught in this same trap. The decline of the U.S. economy will deprive Nigeria and Mexico of the single largest market for their oil. And when the market for Nigerian and Mexican oil dries up, so too will the ambitious but extremely delicate industrial development plans of these countries.

Eventually the Free World's strongest and most advanced countries will begin their own descents into history. Indeed, they may already have begun. For today these countries are in the midst of their own wars against progress. In Japan, for example, environmentalist groups delayed for twelve years the opening of the new Tokyo international airport at Narita. In Great Britain, tax rates have been pushed to such high levels that those few people who do manage to accumulate some wealth usually celebrate their success by emigrating. And the amount of money spent in Great Britain for research and development, when measured as a percentage of gross national product, has been declining steadily since 1961. (The recent election of Margaret Thatcher and her Conservatives suggests that English voters now are firmly on the side of progress. But the enemies of progress have by no means given up, and the struggle in Great Britain is by no means over). In Canada—at least before the election of Joe Clark—bloated government budgets helped push the national inflation and unemployment rates to record levels, while sending the Canadian dollar crashing through the floor to less than ninety U.S. cents. And since 1969, the amount of money spent in Canada for research and development has been declining as a percentage of that country's G.N.P.

Just as in the U.S., opposition to nuclear power is a major component of this overseas war against progress. In 1976, Swedish voters ousted the Social Democrat government of Prime Minister Olof Palme chiefly because that government had announced plans to launch an extensive nuclear-power development program. In Denmark and Norway, groups opposed to the development of nuclear power have successfully pressured their governments to postpone construction of what were to be those countries' first reactors. In The Netherlands, where a recent public opinion poll showed that 55 percent of Dutch voters are unhappy with the prospect of using electricity generated by nuclear power plants, construction of three reactors has been postponed. In Switzerland, a round-the-clock sit-in near Basel forced lengthy delays in construction of a nuclear plant there. In Austria, opposition to nuclear power has forced the government to scrap one plant, in Zwentendorf, and thrown into disarray the government's plans for two more such plants. Similar setbacks have occurred in Belgium and Luxembourg. In West Germany, public opposition has derailed plans to build thirty nuclear reactors that would generate 50 percent of that country's electric power by 1985. France's nuclear power program has been delayed for years by ferocious opposition from assorted environmental groups. And in Canada, opponents of nuclear power are rapidly organizing to stop construction of a reactor in Darlington, which is near Toronto.

Far and away the most dangerous attack in this overseas war against progress is the one which has been launched by the communist parties of Western Europe. Putting aside that argument over how closely these Eurocommunists are linked politically and emotionally to Moscow—the evidence is overwhelming that these links are very close indeed—it is obvious that their domestic economic policies are perfect formulas for disaster. In France, Italy, Spain, and Portugal, Eurocommunist politicians without exception advocate the takeover of their countries' most profitable corporations and most healthy and productive industries. They advocate higher tax rates, major expansions of their countries' transfer-payment programs, and vastly more powerful roles for government in the management of their countries' economies. In short, the Eurocommunists propose to dismantle precisely those programs and policies that carried Western Europe from the rubble and economic chaos of World War II to today's unprecedented levels of material prosperity and social tolerance. They propose to establish programs and policies that closely resemble those now pursued by the various governments of Eastern Europe, and which

147

in one country after another have choked economic growth and made the daily business of living a nightmare of bureaucracy and shortages.

It is not at all difficult to draw a sketch of what our allies' decline will look like. After all, there are not that many ways to sink straight down. Canada will most likely be the first to go under, because of all our allies this country's economic links to our own are the tightest. For instance, more than 65 percent of all Canada's exports are purchased by U.S. customers. And forty-five of the 100 largest industrial corporations in Canada are owned by U.S. corporations. All of this makes it inevitable that as our own economy goes into a tailspin, a major chunk of Canadian industry will promptly go bankrupt. And before long, big corporations in Western Europe and Japan will be falling like dominoes. That's because exports are vital to the survival of most large corporations in these countries, too, and again the U.S. is their most important market. Once we have stopped buying, there is no way they would be able to stay in business by trading among themselves. They are just too small.

Since no two of our industrialized allies are exactly the same, no two will suffer in precisely the same fashion. But in general the decline of the U.S., coupled with the steady escalation of their own domestic wars against progress, will throw these countries into much the same, debilitating spiral that the U.S. will experience—high rates of unemployment, the disappearance of upward mobility, an increase in racial or ethnic tensions, and so forth. Those people who are now poor will remain poor. Those who are already comfortable will become less comfortable. Those who are rich will grow increasingly isolated from their societies and increasingly useless to both their countries and themselves. In each country, the day-to-day business of living will become more difficult, less satisfying. Opportunities will gradually cease to expand, and then they will begin to contract. And as the role of government continues to grow, basic freedoms will begin to disappear.

A tidal wave of political upheaval will wash across the Free World. In West Germany, Italy, and Spain, terrorist activity will increase from its present, very dangerous levels. At the same time, terrorism will spread to France, Belgium, Portugal, Japan, and even to parts of Scandinavia. In Canada, the Quebec separatist movement will flourish under conditions of economic instability. Those factions within this movement that are prone to violence will become impossible to control, and before long the present Canadian confederation will disintegrate into two or more hostile nation-states that will be too weak to flourish or even to survive on their own. And it is more than likely that violent revolutions will take place in those Free World countries that are least able to cope with any significant increases in the level of economic or social strain, such as Italy and Portugal.

In a desperate effort to save themselves, our allies will turn against one another. France will blame its troubles on Great Britain. Great Britain will point an accusing finger at Japan. And everyone will gang up on West Germany. Today's broad political alliance will crumble into a series of smaller alliances that are based not on logic or common sense, but on revived nationalist sentiments and, in some instances, on a misguided thirst for revenge. Economic warfare will break out among our allies as one government after another struggles to save its own workers and corporations by closing the domestic market to competing products manufactured by foreign workers at foreign corporations. For example, Japanese television sets will be taken off the shelves in English appliance stores. French cars will be kept out of showrooms in Japan, and the sale of English airplanes will be banned in West Germany. But this kind of economic warfare—it is called protectionism—will only make things worse as countries that are the victims of protectionist measures retaliate by throwing up trade barriers of their own. As trade among nations grinds to a halt, economic chaos will spread and political rivalries will escalate.

The Soviet Union will not stand idly by while the Free World tears itself apart. Convinced that the collapse of capitalism is in sight, and certain that the final victory for communism is at hand, the Russians will move boldly and decisively to bring about the military disarmament of Western Europe and the political neutralization of its strongest countries. More precisely, the Russians will expand the clandestine programs that even now they operate to train, to arm, and to finance assorted terrorist groups. Moreover, the Russians will vastly increase their already considerable financial support for the communist parties in Portugal, Spain, Italy and France. And to turn the screws on West Germany, where support for the Communist Party is negligible, the Russians will launch a major program to beef up their military forces in Eastern Europe, along the German border.

The Western Europeans will have no choice but to cave in. In the absence of U.S. military and economic power, and in the absence of U.S. political leadership to hold them together as an effective, strong alliance, Western Europeans will quickly recognize their inability to stand firm. Rocked by incidents of terrorism, reeling from the deterioration of their economies, and justifiably frightened by the possibility of a military attack by the Soviet Union, voters in Portugal, Spain, Italy, and perhaps France will reach for the only radical solution to their problems that will be available to them. They will vote the Eurocommunists into power. And when they have done this, these enemies of progress will proceed to implement their programs—and by doing so they will administer the fatal blows. Meanwhile, the West Germans will be left alone to face the Russians. The only alternative to a war the West Germans cannot possibly win, and in any case a war whose battles would be fought entirely on their own densely populated territory, will be to negotiate a political accommodation with the Soviet Union. In other words, the West Germans will be forced by circumstances beyond their control to sign an agreement that in effect will disarm and neutralize them. And the Russians will achieve their most cherished objective—global supremacy—without even firing a shot.

When the war against progress is finally over, the center of international power will shift toward the East. However, the Soviet Union will be only a transitory stop; despite their military victory the Russians will be hobbled by their sluggish economy and by ferocious political rivalries among the more than one hundred ethnic nationality groups that live within the U.S.S.R. In the long run, the center of power will move from the industrialized countries of the West, along with Japan, to those countries in Asia which today are scrambling to set in motion the vital processes of economic growth, technological innovation, and basic scientific research. Countries in this elite category include South Korea, Taiwan, Singapore, and of course China. Indeed, today in these countries both government leaders and ordinary people are beginning to show a faith in progress—a willingness to run its risks in pursuit of its rewards—that has largely escaped the attention of Western observers. Since some of these Asian countries lack basic freedoms as we in the West define them, their rates of progress will be relatively low for the time being. But if these Asian countries continue to pursue progress as doggedly as they are pursuing it today, it is very likely that in years to come they will gradually, if grudgingly, develop the freedoms necessary to roll forward rapidly. They will have no choice but to develop these freedoms.

China will emerge as the world's most dynamic and advanced industrial civilization. Indeed, the wheels have already begun to turn. In May 1978, the Peking government announced plans to launch what may well be the single most ambitious program of rapid scientific and technological development ever attempted by any country. The new Chinese program includes a three-year crash effort in advanced branches of science such as genetic engineering, laser technology, and computer development. In the vital field of energy, the Chinese program calls for the development of ten large oil fields, for the increased mechanization of coal mining, and for extensive research into coal gasification and liquefaction. The program calls for research into solar energy, wind energy, tidal energy, geothermal energy, and atomic fusion. And it specifically includes construction of super-high-voltage power lines wherever they are needed. The Chinese say they will seek to become one of the world's major producers of certain materials that are vital for high-technology manufacturing, such as titanium, vanadium, aluminum, and cobalt. They plan to develop laser technology to use for communications systems, for systems to separate isotopes, and for systems to crush pellets to achieve fusion. And the Chinese program calls for the launching of an undisclosed number of satellites and space-station laboratories.

As we read in the newspapers every day, the Chinese have now begun to implement this extraordinarily progressive program. Today they are in the midst of the greatest effort in their history to import Western technology and equipment. At the same time, the Chinese government has begun to lift many of the ideological and commercial barriers to scientific research and technological innovation that were imposed by Chairman Mao and his radical advisors. For example, under one new program all successful inventors will receive a share of whatever money is earned from the manufacture and sale of their inventions. And finally, in a move that is especially noteworthy in light of China's traditional reluctance to risk exposure to foreign ideas, the Peking government has begun to send hundreds and perhaps thousands of that country's most promising scientists, engineers, administrators, and students to Western universities. To be sure, China's program is too ambitious ever to succeed completely. Setbacks along the way are inevitable, and many plans will be altered in light of changing economic conditions and also to accommodate the never-ending struggle in that country for political power. But when combined with a faith in progress, China's drive and the skill of its people will prove to

153

be an overwhelming force. And as China races forward, so too will her Asian allies. She will pull them forward, just as the U.S. once pulled forward its allies. Eventually it is the East that will dominate the West. It is the East that will be setting the pace, making the rules, calling the shots.

It is important to keep this complex, rather frightening scenario in its proper perspective. It is just that—a scenario. For the war against progress is not yet over. The U.S. is still the world's most advanced, most dynamic, most prosperous civilization. Our decline, and the subsequent decline of our allies, is by no means inevitable. It will happen only if the war against progress is allowed to continue until the enemies of progress have won it. What remains to be seen is whether those of us who believe in progress have the skill and stamina to organize and to mount the kind of counterattack that will put a stop to the present war by openly engaging and then defeating those who are waging it.

8

How to Stop the War

CHAPTER EIGHT

What amounts to a resistance movement has been active for years. At certain times and in certain places, partisans of this movement have stopped the enemies of progress in their tracks. In a few instances, these partisans have even managed to defeat the enemies of progress and to send them reeling back with heavy casualties. Such victories are certainly welcome. However, they are not sufficient. For the war against progress has gone too far, too fast, to be stopped by irregular troops—regardless of how determined and resourceful they may be—who win occasional victories in one place or another. Moreover, a war is not really over when the enemy has been defeated on the battlefield; there is always the danger that he will withdraw to regroup, and then emerge with even more firepower to renew the struggle. A war is over only when the philosophy that drives an army forward has been discredited to the point where it can never again be used to raise an army of sufficient size and strength to pose a serious threat.

To end the war against progress once and for all, we will

need to mount a counterattack that is broadly based, carefully co-ordinated, and clearly articulated. Certainly this counterattack must be designed to defeat the enemies of progress in each specific battle. But more importantly, the counterattack must thoroughly discredit the anti-progress philosophy. To accomplish all this, we will need to do three things: First, we will need to adopt a set of sharp and sometimes brutal tactics for defeating the enemies of progress whenever and wherever they fight to delay or force the abandonment of construction projects that are necessary to make progress. Second, we will need to generate widespread public support for the idea of progress. This will force a steep decline in the number of attacks the enemies of progress will be able to launch. And it will insure that the strength of these attacks will diminish to the point where they will be more of a nuisance than a threat.

And finally, we will need to use our newly-won strength to put our local and state governments—and especially the federal government—back on sensible courses. That is, we will need to eliminate as quickly and as completely as possible those policies and programs that inhibit or prevent progress, and to replace them with policies and programs that will encourage progress and allow it to take place. Obviously, to achieve this last and most important objective supporters of progress will need to win control of our country's major political institutions. In the long run, then, this war will not be stopped on the battlefield. It will be stopped in the ballot box.

A brief look at what the resistance movement has accomplished helps to show just where things stand today. By far its most famous victory came in California, in June 1978. That, of course, was when voters approved Proposition 13, formally called the Jarvis-Gann amendment, to cut property taxes in that over-taxed state by 57 percent. But in fact the California victory was not the first. Back in 1976 partisans of progress in New Jersey rammed a bill through that state's legislature which clamped a limit on the amount of taxes the state could collect. Under pro-visions of this law, the annual budget of the New Jersey govern-ment can grow no more than the personal income of state residents rose during the preceeding year. In 1977, Colorado partisans got a law through that state's legislature which put a 7 percent ceiling on the budget's growth rate. In 1978, Tennessee voters over-whelmingly approved a state constitutional amendment that says the state may not tax or spend at a rate greater than the state's real growth rate. And in Massachusetts, partisans have collected 87,000 signatures to force consideration of a proposal to limit spending by that state's government to a fixed percentage of gross per capita income.

One of the very finest victories for progress has been scored by those members of Congress who fought in 1978 to lower the capital-gains tax. Since the high rates of this tax have long been hampering efforts by entrepreneurs to raise money for new ven-tures, any drop in the capital-gains tax rates obviously would make it easier for ambitious entrepreneurs to raise money they need. Indeed, within a year after the tax rate dropped, there was con-siderable evidence that more and more money was becoming available to bankroll high-risk, high-technology ventures. Nat-urally, the enemies of progress responded to this welcome news by announcing their opposition to any further lowering of the capital-gains tax rates.

By no means has the resistance movement focused exclusively on taxes and government spending. Over the years, partisans of progress have fought and won a number of skirmishes to enable growth and to preserve jobs by neutralizing government regulations. In some instances, these victories have been achieved through the brilliant use of the regulators' own tactics and procedures. For example, back in 1973 a Sacramento-based organization called the Pacific Legal Foundation filed suit against the U.S. Environmental Protection Agency—a refreshing reversal of procedure right there—charging that the E.P.A. had actually violated its own rules. According to the foundation, this violation occurred when the E.P.A. refused to issue a permit allowing DDT to be used in the Pacific Northwest to combat the tussock moth. Officials of the foundation argued that the risks of using the pesticide were negligible compared with the environmental damage done by the moth larvae; the foundation produced evidence to show that during the preceeding year, the larvae destroyed 700 million board feet of timber. Trapped by its own rigid rules, the E.P.A. caved in and granted the requested permit.

Partisans of progress also scored some victories in the November 1978 elections. In Long Beach, California, voters narrowly approved a measure allowing the Long Beach City Council to lease harbor land to Standard Oil Company (Ohio) for construction of a $565-million oil terminal. The terminal would receive and store Sohio's 50-percent share of crude oil from the Alaskan North Slope, for later shipment by pipeline to customers. The Long Beach vote was a key victory in the company's four-year, multi-million-dollar struggle with environmentalists, who oppose construction of the vital storage facility. (Alas, this victory was insufficient to save the project; in March 1979 Sohio announced that it was abandoning the project because the continuing flow of regulatory red tape had made construction of the pipeline economically unfeasible.) Proposals to limit taxes or government spending appeared on ballots in sixteen states. In twelve of these states, the proposals were approved by voters. In Nevada, a property-tax initiative much like California's Proposition 13 was passed by a margin of three to one. In Arizona, voters approved a 7-percent spending limit by an equal margin. In Illinois, an advisory referendum on a spending ceiling rolled up a four-to-one victory. And in Texas, a spending and tax-limit package thundered to victory by a margin of five to one. In New York's Suffolk County, voters were asked to decide whether individual-sponsored initiatives such as the one which gave rise to Proposition 13 should be allowed in future elections; the answer was yes, and by a margin of four to one.

In light of all these victories, it is tempting to conclude that the tide may be turning. Unfortunately, this is not the case. The enemies of progress continue to hold the initiative in this war, and despite the occasional setback they are continuing their rapid drive toward victory. Today more vital construction projects are being delayed or abandoned, than are being completed without interference and on schedule. We are paying more taxes now than ever before, government budgets remain at record levels, and Washington regulators are continuing their efforts to strangle industry by spewing out red tape at an awesome rate. Today's federal program of wage-and-price controls, established by President Carter late in 1978, is an especially devastating blow to progress. Indeed, it is nothing less than a deliberate attempt to undercut the capitalist system and to replace it with a wholly managed economic system in which wages and prices will be set by government rather than the marketplace. And despite some encouraging rhetoric from the chairman of the Federal Reserve Board, the federal government is now condemning us to more inflation in the coming years by continuing its rapid expansion of the money supply. On all fronts, then, it is the enemies of progress who are on the offensive. In each and every theater of this war, it is the enemies of progress who are gaining ground.

And no wonder. The war against progress is at heart an ideological conflict. And it is the enemies of progress—and only the enemies of progress—who have a well defined, clearly articulated philosophy with which to attract supporters. Their philosophy is neat, simple, and at first blush persuasive: There is a natural limit to how much progress a country can safely make. We have now reached this limit. Therefore we have got to stop moving forward before we go too far and bring the whole thing crashing down on top of us. Granted that after careful reflection, this philosophy turns out to be a dangerous and very selfish one. But at least it is a philosophy, which is something that up to now those who believe in progress have failed to articulate. Indeed, look back at each and every partisan victory and it becomes apparent that each of these victories essentially was a negative one. That is, each was fought for and won solely to resist something; to stop a bad situation from growing any worse. Welcome victories? Of course. But not sufficient. Again, the war against progress is at heart an ideological struggle. And in the long run, it is impossible to win a war of this nature merely by opposing the philosophy that gave rise to it. The only way to defeat an army whose power derives from public support for its philosophy is to offer the public a better philosophy.

It can be done. Indeed, it must be done. To borrow a phrase from an earlier struggle, we have got to get out there and win the hearts and minds of the people. More precisely, we must begin to clearly articulate the meaning of progress, to explain the components of progress, and to outline the rewards of progress. And we must warn of the dangers and of the chaos that await us if the war against progress is allowed to continue until its enemies have won it. In effect, the enemies of progress must be isolated by destroying public sympathy and support for their cause. But this is only a first step. Americans prefer to be for something, rather than merely to be against something. So it will not be enough to suggest what they should oppose; we will need to go further and to propose something better for them to support. We will have to offer an attractive alternative to the no-risk, no-growth, let's-share-the-poverty course that the enemies of progress are charting for us. In effect, we will need to articulate, organize, and launch a new political movement whose purpose will be to keep the United States moving forward on its traditional, progressive course. Our movement must be founded on sensible principles. And it must include specific policies and programs to implement these principles and to turn them into reality.

163

Our first principle is that opportunities must always be allowed to expand. For the only way to protect anybody's comfort and security is to increase everybody's comfort and security. The rich can not retain their wealth by keeping the poor in poverty; the strong can not retain their strength by keeping the weak from power. However, this does not mean that the solution is to level out everybody so that we all have the same amount of wealth. You can not make the poor rich by making the rich poor; you can not transfer strength to the powerless simply by destroying the power of the strong. The objective is to add without subtracting, and the surest way to achieve this objective is to allow opportunities to expand as broadly and as rapidly as possible.

The system must keep growing to survive. And the only way to sustain growth is to make progress as fast as we possibly can—by steadily expanding the opportunities of those who are rich to become richer, of those who are comfortable to become rich, of those who are poor to become comfortable. To be sure, growth will often be inconvenient and distressing to those who have already reached affluence, and who must now make room for others. And it will often be risky. But the benefits of growth outweigh its drawbacks, and the alternative to steady growth is wholly unacceptable. Moreover, growth will always be uneven. Some people will always be more comfortable and more secure than others. But the total amount of wealth in a country is more important than the range of wealth in a country. We would rather be unequally rich than equally poor. In the long run, expansion of opportunity will do more good for more people than any effort to achieve equality of condition. As the economic pie itself grows larger and larger, even those with the smallest slices will be able to sustain themselves. Growth helps everybody, just as a rising tide lifts all boats.

Our second principle is that the solutions to our problems will always lie before us, not behind us. We can not solve the problems of the twentieth century by returning to the nineteenth century. Nor can we avoid the problems of the twenty-first century by trying to slow down and to prolong the twentieth century. We will enter the future regardless of whether we want to enter it. Our only choice is whether to march forward under our own steam, or to be dragged forward kicking and screaming all the way. In other words, we have the choice of acting or of merely reacting; of working to guide and thus to control our destiny, or of being at the mercy of our destiny. We prefer to act. And the weapons we will use to minimize the risks, maximize the benefits, and generally to propel us forward along our chosen course are scientific research, technological innovation, and economic growth. Progress will be our strongest shield against danger, our most effective and reliable guarantor of safety.

Our third principle is that good motives are not good enough. We must not allow ourselves to be seduced by public policies and programs that are based too much on nobility of purpose, and too little on sound plans or even on common sense. Indeed we must be very careful never to treat serious problems with cures that are likely to prove fatal. And simplistic solutions that are based solely on the good intentions of those who propose them are inevitably dangerous. They will always do more harm than good. Moreover, we must always bear in mind that a problem is not solved merely

165

because it is recognized and articulated, or even when its cause is accurately identified. A problem is solved by developing a sensibly conceived, carefully organized, affordable program that will ameliorate the problem at hand without also creating an even worse problem to take its place. This approach will inevitably be dull, and often it will seem to be slow. But this approach will always be effective, for it is one that allows sufficient time to pause after each step and to choose the next one carefully. In fact it requires no great genius to understand what must ultimately be done to solve a problem; the trick is knowing what to do next.

Our fourth and final principle is that human beings are the most important species. We must always put the welfare of people before the welfare of plants, of animals, of birds, and of fish. Of course we must be careful never to wipe out lesser species wantonly, or without good cause. But allowing a species of plant, animal, bird, or fish to survive at a cost to our own welfare is more than silly. It is unnatural. It is a direct challenge to the natural evolution of species: a species that can not protect itself does not survive. Human beings are the highest species on earth. We need never apologize for placing our own welfare above the welfare of all the lower species that inhabit our planet. We have the right to do this. Indeed, we have an obligation to do it.

With these principles to guide us, specific policies and programs are fairly easy to establish. Indeed, our policies and programs flow so directly from our principles that they will come as absolutely no surprise to anybody as we tick them off one after another:

Our policy to avoid a crippling energy shortage is to move

166

forward on all fronts. We must continue to rely on nuclear power in the foreseeable future. We must develop new sources of energy, such as synthetic fuel, solar power, and laser fusion power, as rapidly as possible. We must encourage our corporations to dig for coal, and to drill for oil and gas whenever and wherever geologists believe there is a reasonable chance of finding any. And we must develop and deploy technologies that will help us to recover more of these fuels from mines and wells that have already been opened or drilled. To be sure, we must also find ways to use our present energy supplies in the most efficient manner possible. And to do this, we must give our entrepreneurs and our established corporations the incentives they need to develop equipment and machinery that is more energy-efficient than whatever is currently available. But in general, our policy must be to expand the supply of energy rather than to try and avoid a shortage by forcing an artificial reduction in the consumption of it. And we must let our country's corporations do the job, not our government bureaucrats.

Our policy to clean the environment is to control pollution without also destroying our country's industrial base. And the way to do this is to move forward as rapidly as possible with the development and deployment of energy-related technologies. Indeed, the solution to our country's environmental problem is actually contained in the solution to our energy problem. Nuclear power, solar power, wind power, geothermal power, laser fusion power—all of these are cleaner forms of energy than coal, oil, and even natural gas. So the sooner we accept the need for nuclear power, and the sooner our scientists and engineers can develop practical systems for the use of those other esoteric energy sources, the sooner we will be able to clean our environment without also destroying our vitally important industrial base. By continuing the development of nuclear power, and by providing incentives to develop wholly new energy sources, we will actually expand our industrial base as entrepreneurs launch new companies to develop and apply energy technologies, and as the growth of these companies creates new jobs.

We will never be able to clean our environment completely. And we must resist the temptation to try. Pollution is the inevitable by-product of economic growth, and it is impossible to thoroughly eliminate the former without also destroying the latter. It will always be a question of priority; we will always have to choose. And to our way of thinking, the sight of a man who has lost his job because government regulators shut down his factory on the grounds that it polluted, is uglier and less tolerable than the sight of whatever filthy stream those regulators moved in to protect. Of course pure water and crystal air are important. But people are more important, and the surest way to harm them is to take away their jobs or to prevent the creation of enough new jobs for all who need or want them.

Our policy to eliminate the remaining pockets of racial discrimination in the U.S. is to increase the total number of jobs as rapidly as we can. Alas, we will never be able to eliminate all discrimination altogether, for we can not change human nature. But the more jobs we create, the less poverty there will be. And the less poverty there is, the less discrimination there will be. Moreover, the more jobs we create the less painful will be the effects of whatever discrimination does remain on those who will be discriminated against. After all, money is a form of insulation; it hurts less to be disliked when you are comfortable than to be disliked when you are poor. But our goal is to eliminate discrimination as completely as possible. So we must be sure to guarantee the rights of all Americans. Happily, most of the laws we need to guarantee these rights are now on the books. Our policy must be to enforce these laws as carefully and as strictly as we can. For instance, when a Black family that was poor and that had been living in some inner-city slum becomes affluent to the point when it can buy a home in one of that city's suburbs, members of this family must be given full protection by the government if necessary. We need have no sympathy at all for those who might try to drive this family away from their new home. People who discriminate on the basis of race or of religion are more than criminals and bigots; they are enemies of progress too.

To make these policies work, we will need to implement a number of very specific programs. More precisely, we will need to modify and in some cases totally reverse many of those current federal programs whose effects are to inhibit progress or to prevent it altogether. It is scarcely an exaggeration to suggest that the fastest way to achieve a final victory in this war will be to redirect the U.S. government, which today is dominated by the enemies of progress and which serves them as a weapon of incomparable range and power.

We must remove all present disincentives to scientific research and technological innovation. Laws and rules that regulate which experiments may or may not be conducted should be repealed;

these decisions should be left to scientists and to qualified members of the scientific community. We should also repeal anti-trust rules that prohibit our large corporations from pooling their research efforts, and from exchanging the fruits of their individual efforts. Our objective is to achieve as many scientific breakthroughs as we can, as rapidly as possible; the size of the corporations that achieve these breakthroughs, and the profits they might earn by doing so, are of secondary importance.

And we should eliminate the capital gains tax. This will encourage entrepreneurs to launch new, technology-oriented, high-risk companies. Obviously, the more entrepreneurs we can encourage the faster we will be able to increase our country's rate of technological innovation. Less obviously, the more new companies that are formed by these entrepreneurs, the less chance there will be of our largest corporations becoming so large and dominant that they threaten to eliminate all competition in their various industries. Ironically, progress is the best defense against the formation of monopolies.

We must unleash the U.S. economy by peeling the government off its back. Federal income-tax rates should be cut by at least 30 percent. And the tax-rate structure should be changed so that those who earn more money are rewarded for their success, rather than penalized for it. For instance under the present structure corporate profits are taxed twice—once when they are earned by the corporation itself, and again after they have been distributed in the form of dividends to shareholders, who then pay income taxes on this money. This double-taxation should be eliminated. Corporations that earn profits should not be taxed at all on these profits as long as they are plowed back into the corporation to finance research, development, and expansion. Only when the profits are cashed out—distributed in the form of dividends to shareholders—should they be taxed as regular earned income. This change in the tax structure will provide corporations with more available money to grow, and therefore to create new jobs. And this growth will raise the income of shareholders, whose increased abilities to spend will also help to create new jobs.

The federal budget deficit should be eliminated. If absolutely necessary, this could be done by cutting spending. But if tax rates are in fact cut by 30 percent, and if the tax structure is in fact changed to reward success rather than to penalize it, the U.S. economy will begin to grow so rapidly that total tax revenues will increase to cover present levels of spending. Once again, the solution to one problem will contain the solution to another. At the same time, we must put a stop to the irresponsible printing of dollars. The money supply should be expanded at a rate roughly equal to the growth rate of the economy itself. And of course, we must move swiftly to modify or repeal those of our environmental rules and regulations that inhibit or prevent the construction of progressive projects, such as dams and power plants. We should write new rules and regulations that put job-holders at the top of our endangered-species list, and that reflect a more sensible balance than we now have between the need for a clean environment and the need for a healthy, thriving, robust economy.

To contain the most dangerous foreign threat to progress, we must box in the Soviet Union as tightly as we can. For too long now, it is the Russians who have controlled the U.S.-Soviet rivalry.

It is they who have been making the rules and setting the pace. We have obediently been playing their game—agreeing to co-operate whenever they have wanted to co-operate; competing only when they have wanted to compete. This cannot go on. The time has come for the U.S. to seize the initiative. To do this, we must set aside the notion that in the foreseeable future, genuine peace is possible between the two super-powers. The Soviet Union's aggressive behavior around the world, coupled with its continuing arms build-up, make it all too clear that peace is the last thing Moscow has in mind. We must also set aside the notion that whatever their ambitions, the Russians at least will abide faithfully by the terms of any agreements they might reach with the U.S. Nonsense. Angola, the Horn of Africa, Afghanistan, South Yemen —these are just a few countries in which the Soviet government has successfully fought for communist victories, and by doing so broken the implicit code of détente that the super-powers estab-lished back in 1971. And the recent revelation that the Russians have stationed 3,000 combat troops in Cuba is just the latest example of the Kremlin's unwillingness to abide by the terms of its explicit agreements with the U.S.

There is no magic formula for boxing in the Russians. We will have to do it the hard way. Power is the only thing that the Soviet Union understands, and the only thing its leaders respect. The more power that the U.S. has at its disposal, and the more willing we are to use this power when necessary, the less willing the Russians will be to make trouble. So we must abort the strategic arms limitation talks, for the longer SALT continues the weaker we will become. Instead, we should begin to spend heavily for defense. More precisely, we must build the enhanced radiation/reduced blast atomic warhead—the neutron bomb—as quickly as we can, and then deploy it in Western Europe to counter the Warsaw Pact's three-to-one tank advantage over NATO. We must build a new bomber, such as the B-1, to replace our ageing fleet of B-52's. We must push forward now with development and deployment of the Cruise missile. And we must rapidly expand our naval ship-building program beyond its present, alarmingly inadequate level.

At the same time, we must begin to use our economic leverage to weaken the Soviet economy. By doing so we can sharply diminish the Soviet Union's financial ability to sustain its costly weapons programs. For example, we should stop selling the Russians energy-related equipment and technology; without this equipment and technology the Soviet Union will be caught in a painful energy crunch before 1985, and this in turn will help send the Soviet economy into a tailspin. In addition, we will need to take a close, critical look at the present state of our own country's armed forces. Indeed, we must give serious thought to re-establishing the draft. For in terms of both quantity and quality, the U.S. may not be able to defend itself adequately with a volunteer army. Moreover, a country in which most young adults are unwilling to fight except for money can hardly expect a powerful and aggressive foe to take its verbal or diplomatic warnings seriously. The less willing we are to defend ourselves, the more likely it is that we will need to defend ourselves.

And finally, to turn back the Soviet challenge we must unleash the single most powerful weapon in our arsenal: the capitalist

173

system. When fully deployed—when allowed to function without undue interference by government policies and anti-progress activists—the capitalist system brings more genuine satisfaction to more people than any other economic system that has ever been developed. And satisfied people never support the Soviet Union, for it has nothing to offer them. Moreover, because capitalism generates so much wealth it also enables countries to acquire the weapons and machinery that are necessary to resist aggression. So the more wealthy Free-World countries become, the more able they will be to successfully resist Soviet military threats. As leader of the Free World, the sooner the U.S. returns to its traditionally progressive course the stronger our allies' economies will become. Robust economic growth in Western Europe will sharply diminish the political appeal of the Eurocommunists, and their decline will do much to block the Soviet Union from achieving its goal of neutralizing and disarming Western Europe. At the same time, robust economic growth in Western Europe and Japan will help to stimulate growth in Third-World countries by providing bigger markets for their raw materials. And as Third-World economies strengthen, Soviet influence in Asia, Africa, and Latin America will begin to evaporate.

To launch all these progressive policies and programs, we will need to field an army of our own. It must be an army that is strong enough, and smart enough, to decisively defeat the enemies of progress. To do this, obviously, will require money, people, and a talent for organizing both. These are precisely the resources and skills for which U.S. corporations and labor unions are justly famous. And so to a considerable extent, the chances for returning the U.S. to a progressive course will depend on the willingness of business and labor leaders to work together to lead a powerful and carefully co-ordinated counterattack. This is by no means to suggest that business and labor should abandon their traditional adversary roles. Not at all. Hard and sometimes protracted negotiations between management executives and labor union representatives are a vital part of our country's economic system; they have contributed too much to our success ever to be set aside. But if business and labor leaders are unwilling now to form an alliance against their common enemy, they will soon have very little left to negotiate about.

Business and labor leaders will have to fight personally to stop the war against progress. After all, leadership is crucial in any struggle; it is especially crucial in an ideological struggle such as this one. And the enemies of progress have their leaders; we see them on television every evening, we read about them in the newspapers every day, and their writings fill the shelves of our country's libraries and bookstores. They fight hard and they fight well; they lead their troops with courage, skill, and with unflagging enthusiasm. They have earned their victories, and we would be foolish not to admit it and to try and learn from them. But what of those who believe in progress? Where are the natural leaders of this unformed army?

The answer is all too obvious. Up to now the experienced, competent, and in many cases brilliant executives who manage our large corporations and who direct our large unions have remained in the background while the enemies of progress have rolled forward. It is easy to understand their reticence, and to sympathize with them. No one wants to stand up, only to be mowed down by the guns of an advancing army. There is a time to keep one's head down, and a strong case can be made that indeed we have been living through such a time. But there is also a time to climb out of the trenches and to lead a forward charge, even though the risks remain great. And this time has arrived. Simply put, it is now or never.

Business and labor leaders must begin to seek out and engage the enemies of progress on specific battlefields. Today, for example, when most corporations decide to build new factories they announce their decisions as quietly as possible, in the futile hope that nobody except shareholders will notice. This almost never works, and before long the corporation is under attack. From now on, a corporation that decides to build a new factory should go forward with its flags flying, so to speak, and with its big guns blazing. More precisely, the corporation's chief executive, along with the leaders of those unions to which its workers belong, should travel personally to the city or town in which the new factory is to be built. There they should seek out publicity, either by holding a press conference or by appearing at the meeting of some local group such as the chamber of commerce. The forum itself is unimportant.

What matters is that local residents are told—right from the start—what is about to happen and why. The executives and the labor leaders should explain just why the decision has been made to build this factory in this place, how the money to build it will be raised, and from whom this money will be raised. They should explain as precisely as they can just what effect construction of this factory will have on the community—how many new jobs will be created, how much additional money will be pumped into the local economy, just what permanent physical changes will result, and how long it will be before construction-related disruptions can be removed. At the same time, the executives and the labor leaders should explain what would be the consequences of not building the factory—how many new jobs would not be created, how many existing local jobs might disappear, and so forth. Local residents should also be given a glimpse at just how the new factory will affect the corporation itself—what new product it will enable the corporation to market, how much money sales of this new product is likely to generate, how much additional tax revenue is likely to result from the corporation's increased profits. In short, local residents should be offered a good glimpse at how the new factory will fit into the broad scheme of things; of just what role their community will play in the national economy.

It will take a fair amount of time and money to convey this information adequately. Economic growth is too complex a process to be explained in just one morning. So business and labor leaders will have to do a bit of campaigning to make their case. For instance, they should seek out invitations to appear before local community groups such as town councils, planning boards, parent-teacher organizations, and especially local chapters of civic clubs ranging from the Elks to the National Organization of Women. They should make themselves available to local newspapers, and they should appear as guests on local radio shows.

In many communities, it will be helpful to purchase ads in the local papers that will outline the case for the new factory, so that residents may study and absorb it at their leisure. Spot radio announcements will be an especially effective means of communication. One key objective of this campaign is to let residents know that the new factory—or whatever it may be—is the result of a decision reached by real people who have in mind a specific purpose, not by some anonymous, distant corporate entity that is stumbling forward on nothing but momentum.

To be sure, none of this will deter the enemies of progress. They do not scare easily, and they will move as swiftly and as effectively as they can to stop the proposed project. But now, for the first time in this war, it is they who will be on the defensive. It is they who will have to produce facts and figures to counter the ones already placed before the community. Of course, the enemies of progress will do their best to press their case. But now they will find that business and labor leaders are in a strong position from which to wage their own side of the battle. These progress-minded individuals will already be known to local residents, who will have seen or heard them before. And in this kind of struggle, it is difficult to overstate the practical value of recognition. For the first time in this war, those who are openly advocating progress will have it. No longer will the articulate, personable enemies of progress be able to score points against unseen, unknown adversaries. And once this key advantage has been lost to them, the initiative will begin to shift toward business and labor leaders.

With the community behind them, or at least sympathetic to

their point of view, these advocates of progress will be well positioned for their final drives toward victory. For instance, they will find it increasingly easy to convince local government units, such as zoning boards, to grant whatever clearances may be necessary to begin construction. They will find it increasingly possible to win whatever local or state referenda opponents might initiate in hopes of stopping construction. Indeed, for the first time business executives and labor leaders will be able to organize rallies and demonstrations of their own, to counter those which inevitably will be organized by the enemies of progress. And when the battles shift from the public arena to the courts, as they often do, corporations and unions will now be able to call as witnesses scores of people who actually live in the community where their proposed projects are to be built. Such testimony will have a powerful effect on judges and jurors. It will help to convince them that support for the project is widespread, and it will show the enemies of progress for what they really are—a small contingent of elitist outsiders who have arrived to impose their will, and their peculiar point of view, on a community that is perfectly capable of reaching its own decision.

Again, in the long run this war will not be decided in the streets or even in the courts. It will be decided at the polls. The enemies of progress will not be stopped merely by turning back each and every one of their attacks, but rather by forcing a sharp reduction in the number of attacks they are able to launch in the first place. And this means that corporations and unions must do more than merely fight the enemies of progress. They must replace them as well. For too many years now, a majority of business and labor

179

leaders has been discouraging subordinates from running for state and local offices. In a substantial number of corporations and unions such outside political activity is explicitly prohibited. As a result, the profession of public affairs has come to be dominated by individuals who have little understanding of the complex relationships among science, technology, economic growth, jobs, and opportunities. Indeed, the profession of public affairs has come to be dominated by individuals who understand little except how to get elected or appointed to whatever jobs appeal to them. It is really no wonder that our country's corps of bureaucrats and politicians is so deeply biased against progress.

Corporations and unions should encourage their most competent people to seek public office. Young executives and union officials should be urged to campaign for election to local library boards, zoning boards, town councils, and boards of education. Leaves of absence should be granted enthusiastically to executives and union officials who need them to campaign for elective positions, such as mayor and town supervisor, or to accept appointive positions in local, state, or federal agencies. Indeed, a tour of duty in public office should become just as important a part of any corporation executive's or union official's career pattern as a tour of duty in his organization's finance or personnel departments.

Senior executives of our country's major corporations and unions should also throw their own hats in the ring. It is no longer sufficient for these individuals to apply their considerable talents solely to the business of their own organizations. And neither is it sufficient for senior executives to operate behind the scenes, for example by quietly helping to organize political action committees which then enable others to do battle in the public arena. There is a reason why certain individuals rise to the top of their organizations; they are not only more ambitious than everybody else, but also more competent. And today this competence must be brought full force to the profession of public affairs. The objective is to shift the United States back to its traditional, progressive course. To accomplish this objective we will need to build and then to co-ordinate a broad coalition of interest groups that support progress.

A job this difficult can only be done by the very best administrators, the most experienced and effective managers that we have got. And we will find these people in the upper echelons of our corporations and our unions. From now on, business executives and union officials must become more willing to accept political appointments whenever they are offered, such as those to head city, state and federal government agencies. And the chief executives of our major corporations and unions must become more willing to step forward into the political arena itself—to seek election to governorships, to the House of Representatives, to the Senate, and to the Presidency.

Obviously, the struggle to stop the enemies of progress will not be an easy one. And neither will it be a very pleasant one. In effect, it will be a form of civil war. And civil wars are especially nasty. But this particular war has been under way for years, so we are not talking about starting a civil war so much as we are talking about how best to stop one that is already under way. The alternative to counterattacking now is a continuation

181

and inevitably an escalation of the war against progress. For our corporations, for our unions—indeed, for all of us—this would be intolerable. It would mean more misery, more destruction, more chaos than we have ever known. We cannot allow this war to continue until those who started it have won. The question is not whether the enemies of progress can in fact be stopped. They can. The question is whether those among us with the talents and resources to stop them are willing to do it. It is no exaggeration to suggest that on the answer to this question rests the future of our civilization. For a people who are unwilling to defend themselves cannot possibly survive.

CHAPTER

9

The Right Kind of Peace

CHAPTER NINE

We must be careful not to leap from apathy to overkill. We must not let the pendulum swing back so far that our country's forward movement becomes a self-destructive, out-of-control stampede. And it will be up to us—the general public—to make sure that this does not happen. For the war against progress is not a struggle between business executives, labor leaders, engineers, and scientists on one side, versus politicians, bureaucrats, and social activists on the other side. It is our struggle. We the public are not spectators; we are participants. So it is our responsibility to guide this war toward the right kind of peace; a peace that will keep our country moving forward steadily and swiftly—but not recklessly.

For one thing, we must resist the temptation to turn over control of our public affairs to those individuals who actually make progress happen. Of course we must support business executives, labor leaders, engineers and scientists when they launch their projects and when they run for public office. Indeed we must

185

allow them more freedom to operate than we grant them today. But just as war is too important to be left to the generals, progress is too important to be left exclusively to those who make it happen. It is human nature for people in the midst of a struggle to see and to hear only what appeals to them, and to ignore whatever does not appeal. Business executives, labor leaders, engineers, and scientists are especially prone to this human shortcoming, for as a rule these individuals are more determined, more ambitious, and more competitive than most people. So we the public have got to remain deeply involved in our country's public affairs, always on the alert for policies and projects that are too extreme to tolerate. We must devote the time and energy to understand what is truly at stake in economic and political controversies. And we have got to make our own views known by voting regularly.

At the same time, we must resist the temptation to politically obliterate the enemies of progress. There is no guarantor of moderation more effective than a group of individuals who may be counted on to speak out against public policies and projects that are being swept along too rapidly by public opinion. And in our country, the individuals best suited to playing this vital role are those who today are enemies of progress. For they are the ones who—by instinct and by temperment—are most sensitive to the inherent dangers of progress, to the hidden costs of progress, to its unpleasant by-products, to the personal hardships that sometimes accompany progress. They are the ones most skilled at articulating these problems, and at focusing public attention on them when necessary. And the role of critic is especially suitable to these individuals because in general they have no taste for participating

remains to be done. You have got to become more willing to acknowledge shortcomings such as gaps in your data, discrepancies in the evidence, and points of disagreement among experts. As people become accustomed to hearing businessmen, engineers, and scientists readily admit their doubts and uncertainties, people will become more willing to believe these experts when they say that they are sure of something. And when you decide to move forward with specific projects, you should outline not only your objective but also the risks of failure and even the unpleasant by-products of success. In the long run, a willingness to present the complete picture will win the public's confidence, and therefore its support.

You have got to be as absolutely careful as possible. It's true that your safety record is an enviable one; no one who makes an objective study of U.S. industry or American science could possibly conclude that our business leaders, our engineers, or our scientists are in the habit of taking unjustified risks or of moving forward clumsily. But it is clear that in the last few years, the public's sensitivity to risks and clumsiness has heightened. And its tolerance for failures and miscalculations has declined. At the same time, modern systems of communications have fundamentally altered the public's awareness of bad news. There is no longer any such thing as a local or an isolated problem. Whatever happens somewhere is reported everywhere—often incorrectly and, in the nature of news, out of proportion to the whole picture. It goes without saying that this is unfair. But you are never going to change it, so you must learn to live with it. Alas, there is no one suggestion, no one trick, for convincing the public that as you proceed about the business of progress you are doing so with the utmost care. So as you push forward with new technologies and new products, you have simply got to continue to take every reasonable precaution that you can. And as you launch specific construction projects, you have got to take special care that you are proceeding in a way that will do the absolute minimum amount of damage to the surrounding region and, of course, to the people in it.

When mistakes do occur, you must acknowledge them at once and then move with alacrity to correct them. Nothing does more to undermine the public's faith in progress—and its trust in those responsible for making it—than the sight of senior executives heatedly denying that anything has gone wrong in the face of overwhelming evidence to the contrary. It may be incorrect to conclude that an insatiable lust for profit was the cause of the error. But this is the conclusion that many people will reach. And once they have reached this conclusion, their trust will be shattered and their support lost for a very long time, perhaps forever. So as you make your plans, you have got to calculate what can possibly go wrong. And you must decide in advance how you will react if in fact the need arises to take corrective action. In general terms, this means you must be prepared to spend whatever amount of money may be necessary to compensate for a mistake —by recalling a product, by refunding the money people spent for it, by doing whatever it is the victims want you to do. And when an entire community suffers from a mistake or a miscalculation, for example when a factory of some sort spews forth more pollution than its designers had anticipated, you must spend whatever amount of money is necessary to clean up the mess and to

190

compensate for the damage. In the long run, a willingness to pay for mistakes and to correct them voluntarily will increase the public's tolerance of mistakes, and thus its support for progress itself.

And you have got to do more for those individuals who get caught in the gears. Of course it's true that in the long run, progress does a great deal of good for a great many people. But it is also true that from time to time, some very good people are injured along the way through no real fault of their own. For example, the development of integrated circuits has made possible an entirely new electronics industry, which in turn has created thousands upon thousands of well-paying and interesting jobs. But it is also true that booming sales of inexpensive pocket calculators, which use this remarkable "chip" technology, have been a key factor in the recent, perhaps irreversible decline of the slide rule business. And the people who lost their jobs working for companies that manufactured slide rules may not have had an easy time finding new jobs in the growing electronics industry. In this sense, they have been caught in the gears.

To be sure, you cannot allow your sympathies to overrule your judgments. There will always be some element of cruelty to making progress, and the public must learn to accept this if our country is to move forward at all. But today there is no excuse for turning a blind eye toward the personal hardships that inevitably accompany the establishment of new scientific frontiers, the deployment of new technologies, and economic growth. Government hand-out programs such as unemployment insurance and food stamps are not designed—and should not be designed—to

191

rehabilitate working people who get caught in the gears. What's needed are such things as a tax break for businesses that will run re-training courses, and generous tax allowances that will enable workers whose jobs have evaporated to travel around the country in search of new jobs. You should lobby hard for these measures. But even this is not sufficient.

Those of you directly involved in the business of making progress must become alert to the hardships that occur as a result of progressive decisions and activities. You must take an active role in helping those people who have been hurt. For instance, when you choose the location for a new factory or office complex you should take into account the needs of various communities for jobs. And as you hire, you should keep in mind that a willingness to work can be every bit as valuable as whatever specific skill may be required to do the job you are offering. In short, as you make your basic decisions about the withdrawal of old products and services, and the introduction of new ones, you should fold into your calculations the number of resulting hardships in an effort to cause as few of them as possible; you must see not only the people who will be moving forward with you, but also the people who will be left behind.

To those who would make the conversion from enemy of progress to critic of progress—politicians, bureaucrats, social activists, and so forth—we say this:

Set aside your notion that because our system is imperfect, it is intolerable. There is no such thing as a perfect economic or political system; they all have flaws and risks and drawbacks.

Moreover, problems that are wholly the product of these imperfections will develop with an appalling regularity, however carefully and skillfully those who manage the system do their work. It is a cliché to say that the time to really start worrying is when you cannot find anything to worry about; it also happens to be true. Life is trouble, and there is always something to cause distress. Get that big promotion at work, and you have less time to play with your children; win the lottery, and you become surrounded by hucksters scrambling to get a chunk of your winnings. It is much the same for a country. Create more jobs, and the level of pollution rises; lower the price of airline tickets, and making a reservation becomes a major project. No person and no country has ever been or ever will be without a score of bewildering problems to contend with at any given moment. But you must not be discouraged or de-railed by these problems. And above all you must not stop our forward motion in an effort to solve all visible problems before proceeding any further. Just as problems are an inevitable part of life, so too are problems an inevitable part of progress.

Do not be so frightened of the future. Of course the future looks dangerous. It is dangerous. But the future has always been dangerous, and it always will be dangerous no matter what we do. This country was not founded by frightened people. It was not built by frightened people. Our great grand-parents, our grand-parents, and even our parents faced futures that looked, and were, every bit as risky and dangerous as our future looks to us—and is. They did not falter. They did not try to save themselves by stopping progress. They knew their best hope was to keep moving

193

forward. So they did go forward, and by and large they did all right for themselves—and for us. Now it is our turn to keep moving forward. Look around this country and you will quickly discover that the vast majority of Americans is not frightened. Concerned? Sure. Sometimes worried? Of course. But not frightened. So by all means work to guide us safely through the maze of complex choices that lies before us. But do not try to stop us from entering the maze.

Face up to the fact that today's problems are a measure of our country's success, not of its failure. Of course we consume a percentage of the world's natural resources that is disproportionate to our population, and spew out an enormous amount of pollution. We also produce a percentage of the world's goods and services that is disproportionate to our population. Sure it's true that five or ten or fifteen percent of our country's citizens—the percentage depending on which statistics you use—live in unattractive and unhealthy conditions. But these conditions have not developed because of the capitalist system; they have lingered in spite of it. Capitalism does not create poverty, for poverty is a natural state of affairs. Capitalism creates wealth. Indeed there are some fools and crooks among those who own and manage our large industrial enterprises. But again, capitalism does not cause corruption. Greed causes corruption, and so corruption will exist in any system that is managed by human beings. As it happens, the level of official corruption is much lower in capitalist societies than it is in socialist and especially in communist societies. Yes it's true that racial discrimination still exists in our country. But there is less discrimination than there used to be, and there will be less still if only we push forward rapidly with scientific research, technological innovation, and economic growth. By no means does all of this suggest that we should celebrate our country's problems, or even that we should ignore them. It suggests that we must be careful not to propose solutions for these problems that will destroy all we have already accomplished.

And finally, widen your gaze. Start seeing not only those who suffer from progress, but the vastly larger number of people who benefit from it. Start seeing not only what goes wrong, but also what goes right. Start seeing not only the costs and risks of moving forward, but also the much higher costs and risks of trying to stand still and inevitably falling backward. Start seeing not only how far we have yet to go, but also how very far we have already come. You will find little cause for shame, and much cause for pride. For we are quite a country, quite a people, quite a civilization. Despite our shortcomings, our mistakes, our failures, and our occasional catastrophes, the United States has done and is doing a tremendous amount of good for its own citizens and for people around the world. We are history's most successful experiment in human dignity and freedom. To stop progress now, and by doing so to destroy this experiment, would be to trigger history's most horrible calamity.

New York, 1979